The Gourmet Vegan

Heather Lamont is a nurse by profession. Her interest in vegan cooking began when she was entertaining vegan friends. She has won a number of recipe competitions and all the recipes in *The Gourmet Vegan* have been tried and tested on her children — if they disliked them, they didn't go into the book. She lives at Quorn in Leicestershire.

The Gourmet Vegan

HEATHER LAMONT

VICTOR GOLLANCZ

LONDON

First published in Great Britain 1988
by Victor Gollancz Ltd

First Gollancz Paperback edition published 1988
by Victor Gollancz
an imprint of Cassell
Villiers House, 41/47 Strand, London WC2N 5JE
Reprinted April 1993

© Heather Lamont 1988

A catalogue record for this book is
available from the British Library

ISBN 0-575-04377-6

Typeset in Great Britain
by Centracet, Cambridge
Printed in Finland by Werner Söderström Oy

Contents

Acknowledgements

I am grateful to Bill Bingham whose friendship inspired this book and to all my friends who gave me their favourite recipes. Owing to this fact a few of the recipes may not be original; if this is so, I hope that their authors will not be offended. A number of the recipes I have gleaned while travelling abroad.

I wish to thank my husband, Tony, for all his encouragement, along with my children, Rowan and Sharon, for sampling the recipes.

Many thanks to my father for his time spent typing and to my mother for proof-reading.

Also thanks to the many health food shops throughout the country who have happily advised me on the different products, and the Vegan Society who have given me help and encouragement.

H.L.
1988

Introduction

"Tell me what you eat and I will tell you what you are."
Anthelme Brillat-Savarin (1755–1826)

The inspiration to write this book came when I had a vegan friend to stay and discovered first-hand that vegan meals are interesting and tasty experiences, and that vegans themselves are delightful and caring people.

In a society which is predominantly omnivorous, vegetarians in general and vegans in particular are often regarded as cranks. Announcing that one is a vegan invites discussion of the 'Why do you eat apples? You've exploited the worms, insects, bees etc.' variety. But it is their compassionate approach to all forms of life which is perhaps the most appealing part of vegan philosophy.

Veganism is defined as 'a way of living entirely on the products of the plant kingdom'. Vegan cookery, as opposed to vegetarian cookery, uses no animal products at all. This means no meat, fish, poultry, eggs, milk, butter, cheese, or any by-products of animal origin. This definition which appears simple is in fact not so clear-cut and there are grey areas, one of which falls in the realm of sweeteners:

Honey: This is a plant product manipulated by animals and is used by very few vegans. I have therefore not used honey in any recipes.

Sugar: The refining of sugar over animal-bone charcoal has in the past made it unacceptable to vegans. Some refineries now use ion-exchange resins. I have therefore included a few recipes that require refined sugar.

The vegan diet, if properly constructed, is a healthy diet, and the high fibre/low cholesterol content is in keeping with modern medical thinking. Its main disadvantage is the relative lack of iron and vitamin B_{12}. The first can be supplemented by the use of iron cooking-pots but the second requires additional vitamins. Yeast extract, some cereals, and most plant milks are fortified with vitamin B_{12}.

The vegan diet is often criticised as being bland, yet when offering second helpings to a non-vegan guest I have been asked for a nice 'meaty' helping of Vegetable Crumble. A mixture of mushrooms, yeast extract and soya sauce can be mistaken for meat by the uninitiated, and I have included a number of vegan recipes that non-vegan guests will find especially tasty and colourful. These are marked with an asterisk *.

Unless otherwise stated all the recipes in this book serve 4 people; that is the size of my family: however, I have added a chapter entitled 'Eating to Survive' in which the recipes are for one person.

Any recipe that did not pass the 'Did-the-children-like-it?' test has not been included in the book.

A 'Shopper's Guide' which brings you up-to-date on proprietary goods which are vegan, e.g. 'Jus-rol' frozen pastry, and Tate & Lyle sugar, can be obtained from the The Vegan Society Ltd., No. 7 Battle Road, St Leonards-on-Sea, East Sussex, TN37 7AA. Tel: 0424 427 393.

I hope that you will enjoy the recipes in this book.

Conversion Tables

Weight

The Imperial pound (lb) approximately equals 450g – slightly less than ½ kilogram (500g)

Imperial	Approx. metric equivalent
1 oz	25 g
2 oz	50 g
3 oz	75 g
4 oz	100–125 g
5 oz	150 g
6 oz	175 g
7 oz	200 g
8 oz	225 g
9 oz	250 g
10 oz	275 g
11 oz	300 g
12 oz	325–350 g
13 oz	375 g
14 oz	400 g
15 oz	425 g
16 oz (1 lb)	450 g
1½ lb	700 g
2 lb	900 g
2½ lb	1.1 kg
3 lb	1.4 kg
3½ lb	1.6 kg
4 lb	1.8 kg
4½ lb	2.0 kg
5 lb	2.3 kg

Liquid Capacity

The Imperial pint (20 fluid oz) measures more than ½ litre – approx. 575 millilitres (ml)

Imperial	Approx. metric equivalent
1 fl oz	25 ml
2 fl oz	50 ml
3 fl oz	75 ml
4 fl oz	100–125 ml
5 fl oz	150 ml
6 fl oz	175 ml
7 fl oz	200 ml
8 fl oz	225 ml
9 fl oz	250 ml
10 fl oz (½ pt)	275–300 ml
20 fl oz (1 pt)	575–600 ml

Length

Imperial	Approx. metric equivalent
1 inch	2.5 cm
2 inches	5.0 cm
3 inches	7.5 cm
4 inches	10.0 cm
5 inches	12.5 cm
6 inches	15.0 cm
7 inches	18.0 cm
8 inches	20.5 cm
9 inches	23.0 cm
10 inches	25.0 cm

Abbreviations

Tblsp = tablespoon   Dsp = dessertspoon
tsp = teaspoon

* Recommended for non-vegans

Hors-d'Oeuvre

Avocado Purée

> 3 ripe avocado pears
> juice of 1 lemon
> 1 clove garlic, crushed
> salt, pepper
> 1 small onion, grated
> 3 Tblsp olive oil
> 3 Tblsp chopped parsley

Cut open and stone the avocado pears. Scoop them out and mix in with remaining ingredients. Beat to a creamy paste, or blend in an electric blender.

Serve with water biscuits or melba toast (p. 121).

Bhajias or Chilli Bites

> 4 oz wholemeal flour
> 1 medium onion, grated
> 1 tsp ground cumin
> salt, pepper
> 1 Tblsp cake flour
> 1 medium potato, grated
> 1 chilli, chopped to taste
> 1 tsp baking powder

Mix together dry ingredients in a bowl. Add the rest of the ingredients with enough water to make a thick batter.

Take 1 Dsp at a time and drop it into a pan of hot vegetable oil. Fry to a light golden colour, making sure they are cooked inside.

Drain on kitchen paper.

Serve warm.

Variations

Add a cupful of shredded lettuce, or spinach, or watercress to the basic recipe.

Potatoes, bananas, and marrow diced small can be added.

Black Olive Pâté

> 1 lb black olives, stoned
> 2 cloves garlic, crushed
> 2 Tblsp olive oil
> 2 Tblsp dried oregano

Place all ingredients in a liquidiser and blend until smooth.

Check seasoning and add salt if necessary.

Place in an earthenware dish to serve.

Brinjal Pâté

> 2 large aubergines
> 1 Tblsp oil
> 2 onions
> 3 green chillies *or* 1 green pepper, chopped
> salt
> ½ tsp cumin seeds
> pinch caster sugar
> juice of 1 lemon
> 1 lemon, sliced

Rub aubergines in oil and wrap in greaseproof paper and bake for 30 mins. (350°F, 180°C, Mk 4) until soft. Scrape out pulp and mash well. Grate 1 onion and add to aubergine, mix with the chillies or pepper. Season with salt and cumin, and add sugar and sharpen with lemon juice. Chill the mixture.

Turn into a serving dish, decorate with second onion cut into thin rings and slices of lemon.

Variations

Cooked marrow pulp or cooked mashed cucumber may be used instead of the aubergines.

Canterbury Cocktail

> 1 orange
> juice of 1 lemon
> 12 Tblsp cornflour oil
> 2 tsp sugar
> 1 Tblsp chopped mint *or* tarragon
> salt, pepper
> 3 ripe tomatoes
> 2 ripe conference pears
> 4 red eating apples
> 1 Tblsp lemon juice
> sprig of mint

Grate the zest from the orange. Squeeze the juice. Mix together orange juice, lemon juice, oil, sugar, chopped herbs and seasoning. Pour into a deep bowl.

Skin the tomatoes and sieve the pulp into the orange dressing. Chop the flesh and add to the dressing.

Peel, core and chop the pears and 3 apples. Add to the dressing. Chill.

Spoon into 4 dishes. Core and slice the remaining apple, unpeeled, and dip in lemon juice. Arrange on top of each cocktail, sprinkle with orange zest and decorate with a sprig of mint.

Dukkah

> 1 lb sesame seeds
> ½ lb coriander seeds
> ½ lb hazelnuts
> ¼ lb ground cumin
> salt, pepper

Roast or grill the ingredients separately. Finely crush them. If a blender is used do not create a paste. Dukkah is a dry mixture. It will store well in a jar with a lid.

Serve sprinkled over bread slices.

Variations

Instead of cumin use ground cinnamon, marjoram or mint.

Instead of hazelnuts use chick peas.

Grilled Grapefruit

> 2 grapefruit
> 4 Tblsp brown sugar
> 4 glacé cherries

Cut grapefruit in half. Remove white pith centres. Loosen segments. Place sugar in centre of halves and grill under a moderate grill until the sugar has melted.

Serve in individual dishes decorated with a cherry.

Hummus – Method 1

> 6 oz chick peas, soaked overnight
> juice of 2 lemons
> ¼ pt tahini paste
> 3 cloves garlic
> salt
> 1 Tblsp olive oil
> 1 tsp paprika
> 1 Tblsp chopped parsley

Boil the chick peas for 1 hr until soft, drain. Reserve a few chick peas whole. Blend with lemon juice in a liquidiser, a little water may be needed. Add remaining ingredients, and blend to a creamy paste. A sieve or mortar may be used.

Pour the cream into a serving dish. Decorate by dribbling a little red paprika mixed with olive oil over the surface. Sprinkle with chopped parsley and arrange a pattern of whole chick peas on top.

Serve with wholemeal bread or pitta bread.

Hummus – Method 2

> 4 oz chick peas, soaked and cooked
> 1 clove garlic, crushed
> 1 Tblsp olive oil
> 2 tsp tahini
> 3 Tblsp lemon juice
> salt, pepper
> 1 Tblsp olive oil
> 1 tsp paprika
> 1 lemon cut into wedges

Drain chick peas reserving fluid. Liquidise chick peas, with garlic, oil, tahini, lemon juice and enough liquid to purée. Season.

Divide between 4 flat plates, spreading out the hummus to a depth of ½ inch. Indent tops lightly with prongs of a fork. Pour over a little olive oil, sprinkle with paprika and garnish with lemon wedges.

Serve with warm pitta bread.

(You can also serve it with a vegetable casserole. And it freezes well.)

Melon Cocktails

> 1 honeydew melon
> 8 oz lychees
> 4 pieces stem ginger
> 2 Tblsp ginger syrup

Cut melon in half, remove seeds, scoop out the flesh with a melon baller. Reserve juices. Peel lychees and either leave whole or halve and remove stone. Slice stem ginger. Mix together melon juice with ginger syrup.

Divide fruit into 4 small glasses. Pour syrup over the fruit and decorate with sliced ginger.

Miso Spread

> 1 Tblsp miso
> 3 Tblsp tahini
> 2 Tblsp water
> 2 tsp soya sauce
> 1 Tblsp oil
> 1 small onion, chopped
> 1 bunch watercress, chopped

Cream together miso and tahini with the water to make a thick paste. Stir in the soya sauce. Heat oil, add onion and watercress and fry until onion is transparent. Mix all together.

Serve hot on wholemeal toast.

(You can also serve this cold in sandwiches.)

Miso and Spring Onion Spread

> 6 spring onions, chopped
> 4 Tblsp tahini
> 1 Tblsp miso
> 1 Tblsp soya sauce

Combine all ingredients together.
Serve on water biscuits.

Miso and Tahini Spread

> 3 Tblsp tahini
> 3 Tblsp water
> 1 Tblsp miso
> pinch of cayenne pepper

Mix all ingredients together.
Serve on toast.

Tahini and Soya Sauce Spread

> 1 Tblsp tahini
> 2 Tblsp water
> 1 Tblsp soya sauce
> chopped chives *or* sliced tomato

Mix ingredients together.
Serve on water biscuits and garnish with chives or tomato.

Mushroom Pâté

> 1 lb mushrooms
> 2 oz vegan margarine
> 1 medium onion, chopped
> 4 cloves garlic, crushed
> 1 Tblsp miso
> ¼ pt hot water
> 6 oz breadcrumbs
> 3 Tblsp lemon juice
> 1 Tblsp parsley, chopped
> salt, pepper
> grated nutmeg
> sprig of parsley

Wipe mushrooms, reserve 3 for garnish. Chop remainder. Melt

margarine, add onion and garlic and fry until soft but not brown, about 5 mins. Add mushrooms and cook for 3 mins. Dissolve miso in hot water. Add to pan together with breadcrumbs, lemon juice and parsley. Stir over low heat until excess liquid has evaporated. Season with salt, pepper and nutmeg.

Spoon mixture into pâté bowl or 4 small dishes. Garnish with parsley sprigs and raw sliced mushrooms. Chill.

Serve with melba toast (p. 121).

Soups

Soups may sound old-fashioned but they are liked by young and old. They are cheap but nourishing and excellent appetisers. They can be served cold in the summer and hot in the winter.

Vegetable Stock

Vegetable stock can be made from most vegetables. Those to be avoided are beetroot because of their pronounced colour, onions or chicory because of their pronounced taste, and potatoes as they turn the stock cloudy. Vegetables to be used are carrots scrubbed not peeled, cauliflower stalks, cabbage leaves, and vegetable trimmings.

Add vegetables to 2 pt of water and bring to the boil and simmer for 1–2 hrs. Strain. Throw the vegetables away as they are now tasteless and their goodness is in the stock.

Artichoke and Green Pea Soup

> 1 lb Jerusalem artichokes
> ½ lb potatoes
> water, salt for cooking
> 4 oz frozen peas
> 2 pt vegetable stock
> 1 Dsp miso
> salt, pepper
> grated nutmeg
> chopped parsley

Scrub artichokes and potatoes and put in a pan of boiling salt water. Bring back to the boil and simmer for 15–20 mins until tender. Cook the peas for 3–5 mins in boiling water. Drain artichokes and potatoes. When cool peel. Liquidise the vegetables and return to a clean pan. Add the stock and miso gradually, stirring with a wooden spoon, until it comes to the boil. Remove from the heat, season with salt, pepper and nutmeg.

Serve garnished with parsley.

___

Bean Soup

> 4 oz haricot beans
> 4 oz kidney beans
> 4 oz runner beans
> ½ lb tomatoes
> 1 red pepper
> 2 Tblsp oil
> 1 onion, chopped
> 1 clove garlic, crushed
> 1 potato, diced
> salt, pepper
> water to cover
> 1 Tblsp fresh basil

Soak beans overnight in cold water. Drain. Halve runner beans, peel and chop tomatoes, deseed and chop pepper. Heat oil and fry onion and garlic until soft. Reserve 2 Tblsp tomatoes and add remainder to pan with beans, potatoes and pepper. Add water to cover. Season and bring to the boil. Boil rapidly for 10 mins, then cover and simmer for 45 mins, until beans are tender. Add basil and reserved tomatoes and cook for further 10 mins.

___

Beetroot Soup

> 1 raw beetroot, peeled
> 2 pt vegetable stock
> 1 carrot, grated
> 1 onion, chopped
> 1 tsp miso *or* yeast extract
> salt, pepper
> 1 tsp dried dill *or* 1 Tblsp chopped fresh

Dice ¼ of the beetroot and reserve. Grate the rest. Place all the ingredients in a saucepan. Cover and simmer for 25 mins until vegetables are tender. Strain. Add diced beetroot and cook for 8 mins. Sprinkle with dill.

Butter Bean and Tomato Soup

8 oz butter beans
1½ pt vegetable stock
1 bay leaf
2 onions, chopped
1 oz vegan margarine
1 lb tomatoes, peeled and chopped
salt, pepper
1 tsp sugar
chopped parsley

Cook butter beans for ¾ hour in stock with bay leaf.

Fry onions in margarine until soft, add beans, tomatoes and seasoning. Bring to the boil and simmer for 10 mins. Add sugar and liquidise if desired.

Serve garnished with parsley.

Chestnut Soup

1 lb roast chestnuts, skinned
1 onion, chopped
2 stalks celery
2 pt vegetable stock
1 bay leaf
salt, pepper

Boil chestnuts with other ingredients and simmer for 45 mins. Remove bay leaf. Liquidise, and serve.

Clear Vegetable Soup

> 1 ½ pt vegetable stock
> ½ oz vegan margarine
> 1 tsp yeast extract
> 1 bay leaf
> salt, pepper
> chopped parsley
> croutons or
> bread in ½ in. cubes, or
> small pieces of spaghetti or vermicelli

Boil all ingredients together for 15 mins.

Serve garnished with parsley, and croutons or bread or broken pasta.

Cold Fruit Soup

Delicious and popular in the hot summer as a starter or a sweet. The fruit should be ripe and can be overripe.

Fruit stock is made from fruit peel and stones covered with water and boiled for an hour, then strained, and chilled before serving.

Cold Apple Soup

> 1 lb apples
> 2 pt water or fruit stock
> 1 lemon
> ½ lb sugar
> ½ in stick of cinnamon
> 2 Tblsp semolina

Wash and peel the apples, cut into pieces and boil in 1 pt water or fruit stock. Strain and rub through a sieve. Add remaining pt of water or fruit stock. Add the lemon juice, grated lemon rind, sugar and cinnamon stick. Boil for 10 mins. Stir in dry semolina and cook for 30 mins. Take out cinnamon stick. Cool in refrigerator.

(If the soup is to be used as a sweet use 3 Tblsp semolina.)

Cold Plum Soup

> 1½ lb ripe plums
> 2 pt fruit stock *or* water
> ½ in stick of cinnamon *or* ¼ tsp ground cinnamon
> ¾ lb sugar
> 1 lemon
> 2 Tblsp cornflour
> 2 Tblsp cold water

Wash and stone plums. Cook them in the fruit stock or water with cinnamon for 10 mins. Add sugar, grated lemon rind and juice. Remove cinnamon stick. Mix cornflour with the cold water and pour into boiling soup. Cook for further 10 mins stirring continuously.

Cool and serve cold.

Summer Fruit Soup   *

> 2 large cooking apples, peeled, cored and thickly sliced
> 2 firm pears, peeled, cored and thickly sliced
> 6 apricots, stoned
> a few cherries *or* grapes, deseeded
> 6 plums *or* greengages, stoned
> juice of ½ lemon
> sugar
> 1 tsp ground cinnamon

Prepare the fruit and put it in a saucepan with 3 pt of water, lemon juice and sugar to taste. Bring to the boil and simmer for 10–15 mins covered until fruit is tender. You can allow the apples and pears to disintegrate or keep them separate and firm by adding them 5 mins before the end of cooking time.

Place in a serving bowl and dust with cinnamon.

Serve hot or cold with a bowl of small boiled potatoes.

Vary fruit to suit taste and season.

Courgette and Potato Soup

½ lb new potatoes, cleaned
3 courgettes
1 onion, chopped
1 oz vegan margarine
1 pt vegetable stock
1 bouquet garni
1 tsp miso *or* yeast extract
salt, pepper

Dice potatoes. Slice courgettes. Sauté potatoes, courgettes and onions in margarine for 5 mins. Add stock and bouquet garni. Add miso or yeast extract and season. Cover and simmer for 20 mins until vegetables are tender.

Jerusalem Artichoke Soup

1 lb Jerusalem artichokes
1 onion
1 oz vegan margarine
2 Tblsp flour
8 oz tin tomatoes
1 pt vegetable stock
1 strip orange rind
1 tsp yeast extract
pinch of ground mace
salt, pepper
2 oz orange juice
grated orange zest

Peel and slice artichokes and onion. Sauté in margarine until softened. Stir in flour. Add tomatoes, stock, orange rind, yeast extract, mace, and season. Cover and simmer for 15 mins. Remove orange rind. Liquidise the soup. Pour into clean pan, add orange juice and reheat.

Serve garnished with orange zest.

Mushroom and Pasta Soup

3 oz wholemeal pasta shapes
2 stalks celery, sliced
1½ pt vegetable stock
½ lb mushrooms, quartered
2 tomatoes, skinned and quartered
salt, pepper
celery leaves

Cook pasta and celery in stock for 13 mins. Add mushrooms and tomatoes. Season and simmer for 2 mins.

Garnish with celery leaves.

Pea Soup

1 lb fresh peas
2 pt water
1 oz vegan margarine
1 tsp yeast extract
salt to taste
parsley

Wash and shell the peas. Boil the pods in the water for 1 hr. Strain. Use the water for stock, allow to cool.

Add the peas, bring to the boil and cook until tender. Add margarine, yeast extract and salt. Simmer for 15 mins.

Serve garnished with chopped parsley.

Red Bean Soup   *Serves 8*

8 oz red kidney beans, soaked in water overnight
2 onions
2 carrots
other vegetables in season: swedes, leeks, parsnips etc.
2 Tblsp oil
small can of tomatoes *or* ½ lb tomatoes
1 Tblsp tomato purée
3 pt vegetable stock
salt, pepper
bouquet garni
croutons

Drain and rinse beans. Add all the vegetables except the tomatoes, to warm oil in a large pan. Put the lid on and cook gently for 15 mins without browning. Add tomatoes, purée, stock, seasoning and bouquet garni. Boil vigorously for 10 mins. Cook gently for 2–3 hrs until beans are tender.

Serve as a broth or liquidise. Serve with croutons.

Variations

Use dried peas or lentils instead of beans. Or omit tomato purée and add 1 tsp yeast extract. Or use dried potato to thicken.

Rice Soup

    4 oz long grain rice
    1 Tblsp oil
    2 pt vegetable stock
    1 Tblsp yeast extract
    1 carrot
    1 leek
    1 stick celery
    salt, pepper

Heat oil and fry rice for a few minutes until transparent. Add stock and yeast extract. Bring to the boil and simmer for 30 mins. Chop carrot, leek, and celery. Add the chopped vegetables, simmer for further 5 mins. Season.

Vegetable Barley Soup

    4 oz barley
    1 Tblsp oil
    1 clove garlic, crushed
    1 carrot, grated
    3 sticks celery, chopped
    1½ pt vegetable stock
    1 Tblsp parsley, chopped
    juice of 1 lemon
    salt, pepper

Heat oil, add garlic, onion, carrot and celery. Sauté until soft then add stock, barley and parsley and seasoning. Boil then simmer for 1 hr. Stir in lemon juice and serve.

Vegetable Minestra

> 1 carrot
> 1 onion
> 1 parnsip
> 1 turnip
> 2 Tblsp oil
> 1 pt vegetable stock
> 1 tsp yeast extract
> 1 bay leaf
> ½ tsp salt
> ¼ tsp pepper
> 1 potato
> 1 tin tomatoes
> 1 tsp dried parsley
> 1 oz vermicelli

Peel and cut carrots, onions, parsnips, and turnips into narrow strips. Heat oil and fry vegetables until limp, 5 mins. Add stock, yeast extract, bay leaf, salt and pepper. Simmer for 30 mins. Peel and cut potato into strips. Add to vegetables and simmer for further 20 mins. Stir in tomatoes, parsley and vermicelli, simmer for 10 mins.

Quick Vegetable Cream Soup   *

> 1 pt stock
> 2 medium potatoes
> 2 tomatoes
> 1 carrot
> ¼ small cabbage
> few cauliflower florets
> 1 oz vegan margarine
> 1 medium onion, chopped
> ½ tsp yeast extract
> salt, pepper
> parsley to garnish

Wash vegetables and cut into pieces. Place all (except the onion) in the liquidiser together with stock. Melt the margarine in a saucepan and fry the onion until golden. Add the liquidised vegetable and cook for 20 mins. Add yeast extract and salt and pepper to taste. Serve garnished with chopped parsley.

Instead of raw vegetables any cooked 'left-over' vegetables may be used. This reduces the cooking time to 5 mins.

Pea Soup with Mint   *

> 8 oz whole dried peas, soaked and drained
> 1 onion, chopped
> 1 oz vegan margarine
> 3 pt water
> salt, pepper and sugar
> lemon juice
> bunch of mint leaves

Fry onion in the margarine for 5 mins, then add peas and water. Bring to boil, cover and simmer for 2 hrs until peas are soft. Add mint and liquidise. Return to pan and season.

Main Course

Aubergines Stuffed with Nuts

     2 large aubergines
     water to cover
     4 oz mushrooms
     2 Tblsp oil
     1 onion, sliced
     4 oz mixed nuts
     4 oz breadcrumbs
     1 Tblsp yeast extract
     ½ tsp marjoram
     salt, pepper
     ½ oz vegan margarine
     chopped chives

Add aubergines to a pan of boiling water to cover and parboil for 10 mins. Drain and cool. Cut them in half lengthways. Scoop out the flesh carefully, keep flesh and skins.

Chop mushrooms. Heat oil and fry onion until brown. Add nuts and 3 oz breadcrumbs and cook until breadcrumbs are crisp. Stir in the mushrooms and yeast extract and continue to cook for 5 mins. Combine with the aubergine flesh, marjoram, and seasoning.

Arrange the 4 skins in an ovenproof dish. Divide the filling between them. Sprinkle with remaining breadcrumbs and dot with margarine. Bake for 20 mins (375°F, 190°C, Mk 5).

Serve garnished with chives.

Aduki Bean, Carrot and Ginger Stir-Fried

> 4 oz Aduki beans, soaked, cooked and drained
> 1 onion, sliced
> 4 Tblsp oil
> 1½ lb carrots, sliced thinly
> 1 Tblsp grated fresh ginger
> ½ pint water *or* vegetable stock
> spring onions, chopped
> 1 tsp sugar
> 1 Tblsp arrowroot
> 4 Tblsp soya sauce
> salt, pepper

Fry onion in hot oil for 2 mins. Add carrots and ginger and stir-fry for further 3 mins. Add aduki beans and water, cover and simmer for 10 mins. Stir in spring onions. Dissolve sugar and arrowroot in soya sauce and add, stirring all the time. Season to taste.

Serve with rice and salad.

Artichokes with Mushrooms

> 4 globe artichokes
> water to cover
> ½ lb flat mushrooms
> 1½ oz vegan margarine
> 1 carrot, chopped
> 1 onion, chopped
> 2 Tblsp parsley, chopped
> 1 Tblsp chopped mixed herbs *or* 1 Dsp dried mixed herbs
> 4 Tblsp breadcrumbs
> ¼ pt white wine
> ½ pt vegetable stock
> flour
> salt, pepper

Trim artichokes. Place in boiling salt water to cover and cook for 20 mins until leaf can be pulled out. Drain, leave to cool. Wash and chop mushrooms. Reserve 4 whole ones.

Melt margarine, put in carrot and onion and cook slowly to soften them, then add mushrooms. Cook for 5 mins. Add parsley, herbs and enough crumbs to make a moist mixture.

Pull out centre leaves of artichoke and carefully scrape out the chokes. Divide the mushroom mixture and fill the centre of the artichokes. Top each with a whole mushroom. Arrange in a deep ovenproof dish, pour around the white wine and stock. Cover with foil and cook for 35 mins (350°F, 180°C, Mk 4). Pour off the liquid and thicken with a little flour to make a sauce. Season sauce and pour around artichokes.

Bean and Tomato Hot-Pot

    15 oz tin red kidney beans, drained
    14 oz tin tomatoes
    2 Tblsp oil
    2 onions, sliced
    3 carrots, sliced
    2 sticks celery, sliced
    1 large leek, sliced
    2 cloves garlic, crushed
    ½ pt vegetable stock
    1 Tblsp yeast extract
    salt, pepper
    1½ lb potatoes, sliced
    ½ oz vegan margarine

Heat oil. Fry onion for 5 mins. Add carrots, celery, leek and garlic and fry for 5 mins. Add kidney beans, tomatoes and juice, stock, yeast extract and salt and pepper to taste. Mix well.

Place in casserole dish. Arrange potatoes over top and sprinkle with salt and pepper, dot with margarine and cover. Place in oven (350°F, 180°C, Mk 4) for 2 hrs. Remove lid for last 30 mins to brown potatoes.

Bean Provençal   *

    6 oz kidney beans
    2 Tblsp oil
    3 oz mushrooms, sliced
    1 leek, sliced
    1 clove garlic, crushed
    14 oz tin tomatoes
    1 tsp mixed herbs
    1 Dsp miso
    ¼ pt vegetable stock
    salt, pepper

Soak beans overnight in plenty of cold water, rinse. Place in pan with salted water and bring to the boil. Cover and boil rapidly for 10 mins. Drain, discard water.

Fry mushrooms, leeks and garlic in oil for 5 mins. Add tomatoes, herbs, seasoning, miso and stock. Add beans, cover, and simmer for 30 mins.

Serve with rice or pasta and salad.

Butter Beans and Celery

½ lb pre-cooked butter beans
2 sticks celery, sliced
1 onion, sliced
1 bay leaf
1 Tblsp chopped parsley
1 Tblsp soya milk
1 large tomato, skinned and sliced
salt, pepper
1 Tblsp sugar
¼ oz vegan margarine
Sauce
1½ oz vegan margarine
1 oz flour
½ pt soya milk

Put beans, celery, onion and bay leaf in a pan. Cover with boiling water. Season and simmer for 30 mins.

Make a white sauce. Melt margarine, add flour and cook for 1 min, add soya milk slowly stirring all the time, bring to the boil until sauce thickens.

Drain vegetables. Reserve ¼ pint of liquid. Remove bay leaf.

Add vegetables to white sauce, mix gently, add parsley, soya milk and reserved liquid. Season to taste. Turn into a shallow dish.

Dust tomato slices with salt, pepper, sugar, and margarine. and grill. Arrange them on top of the beans. Serve.

Butter Beans with Apricots, Cinnamon and Almonds

Serves 2–3

    4 oz dried butter beans, soaked, cooked and drained
    1 onion, chopped
    2 Tblsp oil
    2 tsp cinnamon
    4 oz dried apricots, sliced
    1½ oz raisins
    ¾ pt water
    1 oz coconut cream
    1 Tblsp lemon juice
    salt, pepper
    2 oz almonds, flaked and toasted

Fry onion in oil for 10 mins. Stir in cinnamon and cook for 1 min. Add beans, apricots, raisins and water. Bring to the boil, then simmer, covered, for 20 mins until apricots are tender. Add coconut cream, lemon juice and seasoning. Sprinkle almonds on top before serving.

Serve with rice and salad.

It can also be used as an accompaniment to a curry when it will serve 4–6.

(It freezes well.)

Butter Beans with Tomatoes and Green Peppers

    8 oz butter beans, cooked
    2 onions, chopped
    1 oz vegan margarine
    2 cloves garlic, crushed
    2 green peppers, sliced
    1 lb tomatoes, skinned and chopped
    1 Tblsp tomato purée
    salt, pepper

Fry onions in margarine for 10 mins. Add garlic, peppers, tomatoes and tomato purée. Cook for 15 mins stirring often. Add butter beans and season to taste. Cover, and simmer for 10 mins.

Serve with rice, noodles, bread, or boiled or jacketed potatoes.

(It freezes well.)

Red Beans with Rice and Vegetables

4 oz red kidney beans, cooked
2 onions, chopped
2 cloves garlic, crushed
4 Tblsp oil
12 oz rice
1 Tblsp turmeric
1½ pt water
salt, pepper
4 carrots, diced
2 courgettes, sliced
1 red pepper, chopped
4 tomatoes, skinned and chopped

Fry onion and garlic in oil for 5 mins. Stir in rice and turmeric. Add water and seasoning. Bring to the boil and simmer for 20 mins. Add carrots, DO NOT stir, cook for 10 mins. Add courgettes, pepper, tomatoes and beans without stirring, cook for 10 mins. Remove from heat and leave to stand for 15 mins.

Mix gently with a fork and serve with a salad.

(It freezes well.)

Brown Lentil Burgers

12 oz continental *or* brown lentils, soaked and drained
1 bay leaf
1 onion, chopped finely
2 Tblsp soya flour
1 Tblsp tomato purée
salt, pepper
4 Tblsp parsley, chopped
1 tsp cumin
1 tsp yeast extract
wholemeal flour for coating
oil for shallow frying

Put lentils and bay leaf into a saucepan, cover generously with water and bring to the boil. Boil for 10 mins, then simmer gently for 45 mins until tender. Drain and remove bay leaf. Add remaining ingredients and mix well. Form into burgers, coat with flour, shallow fry over moderate heat until crisp on both sides.

Serve with salad and pickle between warm wholemeal rolls.

Burghul Pilav

> 1 lb cracked wheat (burghul)
> 8 oz vegan margarine
> 1 onion, chopped
> salt
> 1 pt vegetable stock
> 1 tsp yeast extract

Melt 4 oz margarine in a heavy saucepan, fry chopped onion until soft. Add burghul and fry lightly for 10 mins, stirring all the time. Season to taste and add yeast extract. Pour over stock to cover by about ½ in. Mix well and simmer over low heat for 10 mins.

Melt remaining margarine and pour over burghul. Place greaseproof paper over pan and put on a tightly fitting lid. Leave over lowest heat for ½ hour.

Serve instead of rice with vegetable stews.

Variations

2 tsp of chopped nuts or tofu, cut into cubes, or fried aubergine cubes, stirred in at the end.

Chow Mein with Tofu

> 1 lb noodles
> 1 pt water, 4 Tblsp water
> 1 onion
> 1 green pepper
> ½ med. white cabbage
> 4 oz mushrooms
> ½ bunch watercress
> 1 Tblsp arrowroot
> 2 Tblsp soya sauce
> ½ tsp sugar
> 3 Tblsp oil
> 3 oz vegetable fat
> 4 oz tofu
> 4 oz bean sprouts

Boil noodles in a pint of water for 8 mins and drain.

Chop onion, green pepper, shred cabbage, slice mushrooms,

wash watercress and remove stems. Mix arrowroot in a bowl with the soya sauce, sugar and 4 Tblsp water to a runny consistency.

Heat 2 Tblsp oil and 2 oz fat in a pan until hot. Stir-fry the onions and peppers for 3 mins. Drain the tofu – if necessary, chop it into matchstick size, add to the pan, and fry for 2 mins. Add cabbage, watercress and mushrooms and stir-fry for 2 mins. Add bean sprouts and arrowroot mixture and simmer for 3 mins.

Remove half the vegetable mixture and put on one side.

To the remaining half add the noodles and stir-fry for 3 mins, until noodles are heated through. Transfer to a hot serving dish. Return reserved vegetables to pan with 1 Tblsp oil and 1 oz vegetable fat. Stir-fry for 3 mins until sauce thickens. Place on top of noodles.

Serve with a salad.

Chow Mein with Vegetables

> 1 lb noodles
> 1 pt water, 4 Tblsp water
> 4 Tblsp vegetable oil
> 4 oz vegetable fat
> 1 tsp ground ginger
> ½ head celery, diced
> ½ cabbage, diced
> 2 onions or leeks, sliced
> 2 carrots, sliced
> ½ pt vegetable stock
> 1 tsp yeast extract
> 1 Tblsp soya sauce
> 2 Tblsp cornflour
> salt
> ¼ lb bean sprouts, or 1 can, drained

Boil noodles in 1 pt water for 8 mins. Drain.

Heat 3 Tblsp oil and 3 oz fat in a pan until hot. Add the ginger and all the vegetables except the bean sprouts and stir-fry for 3 mins. Add the stock and bring to the boil. Simmer for 5 mins. Add the yeast extract and soya sauce. Mix the cornflour with 4 Tblsp water and add, stirring all the time. Season to taste.

Remove half the vegetable mixture and put on one side.

Add the noodles to the remaining half and stir-fry for 3 mins, until the noodles are heated through. Transfer to a hot serving dish. Return the reserved vegetables to the pan with 1 Tblsp oil and 1 oz fat. Add the bean sprouts and cook for further 2 mins. Place on top of the noodles.

Serve with a salad.

Croustade of Mushrooms   *

Croustade
4 oz breadcrumbs
4 oz ground almonds/hazel nuts
2 oz vegan margarine
4 oz flaked almonds
1 clove garlic, crushed
½ tsp mixed herbs

Topping
1 lb mushrooms
2 oz vegan margarine
2 Tblsp flour
½ pt soya milk
4 tomatoes, skinned and sliced
1 Tblsp chopped parsley
salt, pepper and nutmeg

Mix breadcrumbs and ground nuts, rub in margarine. Add flaked almonds, garlic and herbs, mix well. Press down very firmly into large greased ovenproof 9-in dish. Bake in oven (450°F, 250°C, Mk 8) for 15 mins.

Sauté mushrooms in margarine. Add flour, stir in soya milk and reheat, stirring until it thickens. Simmer for 10 mins and season with salt, pepper and nutmeg. Spoon mushroom sauce over top of croustade.

Top with tomatoes, return to oven for 10–15 mins.

Serve garnished with parsley.

Courgettes or Aubergines with Tomatoes

> 1½ lb courgettes *or* aubergines *or* both
> 1 clove garlic, crushed
> 4 Tblsp olive oil
> ¾ lb tomatoes, skinned and chopped
> 2 Tblsp parsley, chopped
> salt, black pepper

Cut the courgettes or aubergines into thick rounds. Sprinkle with salt and leave to drain in a colander for ½ hr. Squeeze aubergines dry.

Sauté gently with crushed garlic in olive oil, turn the slices until soft. Add tomatoes and squash them gently. Sprinkle with parsley, season to taste and simmer until well cooked.

Serve hot with rice or burghul.

(This can also be served cold as an hors d'oeuvre.)

Dolmades

> 1 Savoy cabbage
> 4 Tblsp rice
> 1 medium onion, chopped
> 2 oz vegan margarine
> 4 oz mushrooms, chopped
> 1 small tin sweetcorn, drained
> ½ lb tomatoes, skinned
> 1 Dsp tomato purée
> 1 Dsp wholemeal flour
> ½ pt vegetable stock

Boil rice in salt water for 10 mins until soft.

Wash cabbage, trim off stalks. Put in a large pan and boil for 3 mins. Lift out and begin to peel off the leaves. As soon as they become difficult to remove, put the cabbage back into the boiling water, until all the bigger leaves are detached. Chop the cabbage heart and include in the filling.

Melt 1 oz margarine and fry the onion for 3 mins. Add the mushrooms and fry for 2 mins. Remove and turn into a bowl with the rice and sweetcorn. Spread out each leaf and add 1 Dsp of filling, roll up each leaf like a parcel. Place in a casserole dish and lightly dust with flour. Pour over stock and bake for 20 mins (350°F 180°C, Mk 4).

Drain stock and use to make sauce.

Alternative Filling

> 2 onions, chopped
> 4 oz wholemeal breadcrumbs
> 1 Tblsp soya sauce
> 8 oz tin pineapple pieces, drained
> 4 oz walnuts, chopped
> juice of 1 lemon
> 4 tomatoes, skinned and chopped

Mix all ingredients together, place on cabbage leaves, and proceed as before.

Tomato Sauce

Melt 1 oz margarine, add flour and cook for 1 min. Add stock and stir until thickened. Add tomato purée. Slice tomatoes into wedges, add to sauce and spoon over dolmades.

Falafel

Makes 18

> 6 oz dried chickpeas, soaked *or* 2 x 14½ oz tins cooked
>   chickpeas
> water
> 1 onion, chopped
> 2 cloves garlic, crushed
> ½ tsp black pepper, ground
> ½ tsp turmeric, ground
> 2 tsp cumin, ground
> 2 tsp coriander, ground
> salt
> 2 tsp parsley, chopped
> 2 Tblsp oil

If dried chickpeas are used, put them in a pan, cover with water and bring them to the boil. Simmer for at least 2 hours until soft. Top up water if necessary.

Drain the tins of cooked chickpeas or cooked dried chickpeas.

Mash or liquidise them, adding a little water if the mixture becomes dry.

Stir in the onion, garlic, spices, seasoning and parsley, then form the mixture into 18 cylinder shapes. Chill for 30 mins. Fry in a lightly oiled pan until brown all over.

Serve with pitta bread and a salad.

(Falafel freeze well.)

Khitchari

> 1 onion, chopped
> 4 cloves garlic, crushed
> 1 tsp turmeric
> 1 tsp ground ginger
> ½ tsp curry powder
> 1 tsp ground cumin
> 3 Tblsp oil
> 6 oz potatoes, peeled and diced
> 8 oz mung beans, soaked and drained
> 8 oz rice
> 1¾ pt water
> 2 Tblsp lemon juice
> salt, pepper

Fry onion, garlic and spices in oil for 10 mins. Stir in potatoes, beans and rice. Add water and bring to the boil. Cover and cook for 45 mins. Turn off heat and leave to stand for 15 mins, until liquid is absorbed. Add lemon juice and seasoning.

This is an Indian dish, serve with pappadums and a tomato and onion salad.

If a little dry, a tomato and basil sauce (p.60) or liquidised ratatouille sauce can be served.

(This dish freezes well.)

Lentil and Tofu Roast

> 1 lb cooked lentils
> 8 oz tofu, crumbled
> 1 onion, chopped
> 1 tsp mixed herbs
> 1 tsp cayenne pepper
> 2 Tblsp oil
> salt

Sauté onion in oil, combine all the ingredients.

Place in greased casserole dish. Cover and bake for 30 mins at 350°F, 180°C, Mk 4. Uncover and bake for a further 15 mins. Serve hot or cold with a salad.

Lentil and Vegetable Stew

> ½ lb lentils, soaked overnight, drained
> 1 pt water
> 2 potatoes, peeled and diced
> ½ lb courgettes *or* marrow, cubed
> ½ lb leeks, sliced
> 1 stalk celery, sliced
> salt, pepper
> 1 onion, chopped
> oil
> 2 cloves garlic, crushed
> 2 Tblsp parsley, chopped
> juice of 2 lemons

Simmer lentils in a large pan in 1 pt of water for 1¼ hrs until nearly soft. Add potatoes, courgettes, leeks and celery, season to taste and cook for a further 15 mins until vegetables are cooked. Add more water if necessary. Only a little fluid should be left.

Fry onion in oil until soft. Add garlic and fry for 2 mins. Drain and add to lentils and vegetables together with parsley and lemon juice. Simmer for a few minutes.

Serve hot or cold.

Onion and Apple Pie

    8 oz wholemeal pastry
    2 onions, sliced
    1 lb cooking apples, peeled, cored and sliced
    salt, pepper
    1 tsp sage, chopped
    pinch mixed spice
    1 oz thinly sliced vegan margarine

Set oven at 400°F, 200°C, or Mk 6.

Roll out half pastry to line 7-in flan dish.

Blanch the onions and drain them. Put a layer of apples on the flan, and a layer of onions, season and add sage and spice. Cover with apple to fill the flan. Cover with slices of margarine.

Roll out the rest of the pastry to cover the flan, seal edges, trim and decorate. Bake for 35 mins.

Serve hot.

Paella

    8 oz rice
    4 Tblsp oil
    3 onions, chopped
    1 clove garlic, crushed
    1 tsp turmeric
    3 tomatoes, skinned and chopped
    1 pt vegetable stock
    2 stalks celery, chopped
    1 red pepper, sliced
    4 oz peas
    1 Tblsp parsley, chopped
    1 tsp marjoram
    2 Tblsp cashew nuts
    rind and juice of 1 small lemon
    1 Tblsp soya sauce
    salt, pepper

Fry rice in oil until yellow. Add onions, garlic and turmeric and fry for a few mins. Add tomatoes and stock. Boil and simmer for 5 mins. Add celery, pepper and peas. Simmer until rice is cooked. Stir in herbs, nuts, lemon rind and juice, soya sauce and salt and pepper.

Serve hot.

Pizza

Serves 6–8

Tomato Topping
1 tin tomatoes
2 Tblsp tomato purée
1 tsp sugar
1 medium onion, chopped
2 tsp dried oregano
salt, pepper

Scone Base
8 oz self-raising flour
1 tsp baking powder
1 tsp salt
1 oz vegan margarine
¼ pt water
2 Tblsp prepared mustard

Prepare the tomato topping. Put all the ingredients including the juice from the tin of tomatoes in a pan. Season with salt and pepper. Cook gently for 30 mins without a lid until the mixture reduces to a thick pulp.

While the tomato mixture is cooking, make the base. Sift the flour, baking powder and salt into a bowl. Rub in the margarine and mix to a soft dough with the water. Turn on to a large baking sheet. Roll out to a 10 in. circle for the pizza base. Spread the mustard evenly over the base. When the tomato mixture is cooked spread it over the dough to within 1 in. of the edge. Decorate the top with a variety of the following:

parsley	sliced mushrooms
marjoram	celery, chopped
oregano	capers
basil	black olives
onion rings	sliced green and red peppers
sliced tomatoes	

Bake at 400°F, 200°C, Mk 6, for 30–40 mins, until well risen and brown round the edges.

Serve hot with a tossed green salad.

Stuffed Jacketed Potatoes

>4 medium old potatoes
>4 oz mushrooms
>1 small onion
>1 oz vegan margarine
>salt, pepper

Wash potatoes, prick skin with a fork, wrap in foil. Bake at 350°F, 180°C, Mk 4 until tender, about 1 hr.

Dice mushrooms and onions. Fry in margarine until cooked.

Cut potatoes in half. Scoop out centre and mash. Mix mushrooms, onions, seasoning and potatoes together and return to skins.

Reheat in oven.

Carrot and Almond Filling

>2 large carrots
>1 oz vegan margarine
>2 oz flaked almonds
>1 tsp grated orange rind
>pinch of raw sugar
>salt, pepper

Peel and slice carrots and parboil. In a separate pan melt margarine and add almonds, orange rind, sugar and salt and pepper. Cook over low heat for a few mins, stirring continuously. Drain carrots and put them in the sauce, cook for 5 mins, basting frequently.

Slit the cooked potato and pour the sauce over.

Tomato and Bean Filling

>4 tomatoes *or* 14 oz tin
>10 oz cooked kidney beans
>1 onion
>1 pepper
>1 stick celery
>1 Tblsp oil
>1 tsp chilli powder
>salt, pepper

Chop onion, pepper, celery and sauté in margarine until tender. Drain the tomatoes and reserve the juice. Dice canned or fresh tomatoes and stir into the mixture with the beans, chilli powder and seasoning. Add a little juice or water and simmer for 30 mins until reduced to a thick sauce.

Split the potatoes and pour the sauce over.

Olive Filling

> 4 oz mushrooms
> 1 oz vegan margarine
> 12 stuffed olives
> salt, pepper

Chop mushrooms and sauté in margarine until tender. Slice the olives and mix them into the mushrooms, season. Slit the potatoes open in a cross and put a spoonful of filling inside each. Keep hot in the oven until served.

Pakora

> 8 oz chickpea flour
> 2 tsp cumin, ground
> pinch of cayenne pepper
> salt
> a little cold water
> okra, cut while dry
> 2 lb vegetables in season:
>> carrots, broccoli, small Brussels sprouts, cauliflower, courgettes, aubergines, mushrooms, parsnips
> oil for deep frying

Beat together flour, spices, salt and pepper. Add enough water to give batter consistency of a smooth, thin white paste. Chill batter for 1 hour at least.

Prepare vegetables and cut them into strips, slices, or florets. Heat oil in deep pan until it spits when batter is dropped in. Dip vegetables one at a time in batter and coat all over. Drop into fat and cook until golden. Root vegetables take longer to cook. Drain and keep warm.

Serve with chutneys, pickles and soya sauce.

Ratatouille

In Method 1 the aubergines stay whole; in Method 2 they become a pulp.

Method 1

3 Tblsp oil
2 large onions, sliced
2 red or green peppers, sliced
2 aubergines, diced
4 tomatoes, sliced
1 clove garlic, crushed
salt, pepper
2 Tblsp chopped parsley, thyme and basil

Heat oil, add onions and cook gently. When soft add peppers, then aubergines, then tomatoes. Add garlic and seasoning. Stir gently. Cover with a tight lid. Cook slowly on top or in the oven for 20–30 mins. Shake the pan occasionally, do not remove the lid.

Serve hot with rice.

('Left-overs' can be served as a salad, or liquidised and used as a spread or in gravies. It freezes well.)

Method 2

2 aubergines
½ lb courgettes
1 large green pepper
4 Tblsp olive oil
½ lb tomatoes or 14 oz tin
2 small onions, sliced into rings
2 cloves garlic, chopped
1 large red pepper
salt, pepper

Slice and salt aubergines and courgettes and leave to stand. Scald, skin, deseed and slice tomatoes, or drain tinned tomatoes. Halve peppers, core, deseed and cut into strips.

Heat oil in a stewpan and fry onion and garlic for 2 mins. Wipe dry aubergines and courgettes. Add to pan and fry for 3 mins each side, add extra oil if needed. Season the mixture. Add peppers and tomatoes and cover tightly, cook gently for 1 hr.

Ratatouille should be a soft rich mass.

Sweetcorn Ratatouille   *

> 1 large aubergine
> 1 large red or green pepper
> 1 onion
> 1 courgette
> 3 large tomatoes
> 3 Tblsp oil
> 1 clove garlic, crushed
> 4 oz can sweetcorn
> 1 bay leaf
> salt, pepper
> 2 oz walnut pieces
> parsley to garnish

Dice the aubergine, sprinkle with salt and leave for 30 mins. Slice the pepper and onion into thick strips. Slice courgette into ½ in chunks. Chop the tomatoes.

Heat oil in a pan. Add garlic, onion and peppers. Fry for 5 mins, stirring all the time.

Rinse and dry the aubergine. Add to the pan with the courgette. Cook for 10 mins.

Add tomatoes, drained sweetcorn, bay leaf and salt and pepper. Cover pan and simmer for 10 mins until vegetables are just cooked. Remove bay leaf. Stir in walnuts. Sprinkle with parsley.

Serve with jacketed potatoes, rice or pasta.

Rice and Carrots

> 1 lb cooked rice
> 1 onion, chopped
> 2 Tblsp oil
> 1 lb carrots, grated
> 1 Tblsp sugar
> ½ tsp ground cinnamon
> salt
> juice of 1 orange

Fry onions in oil until soft. Add carrots, sugar, cinnamon and salt and sauté for 10 mins.

Oil a casserole dish. Spread alternate layers of rice and

carrots in the dish, starting and ending with rice. Pour orange juice over and bake at low heat (350°F, 180°C, Mk 4) for 30 mins with tightly covered lid.

Hawaiian Fried Rice

> 8 oz cooked rice
> 3 oz vegan margarine
> 4 oz chopped onions
> chopped chives
> 8 oz diced celery
> 4 oz sliced mushrooms
> 1 Tblsp yeast extract
> 2 Tblsp soya sauce
> 8 pineapple rings
> salt, pepper

Heat margarine in frying pan. Add onions, chives and celery and cook until almost tender. Add mushrooms, rice, yeast extract and soya sauce. Cook for 10 mins over low heat. Heat pineapple rings.

Serve mounds of this savoury rice on the pineapple rings.

Mexican Rice

> ½ lb rice
> 2 oz oil
> ¾ pt water
> 1 onion, chopped
> 1 green pepper, chopped
> 2 oz tomato purée
> salt, pepper
> piri-piri to taste
> a few onion rings and green pepper rings to garnish

Sauté rice in oil until golden. Add water, onion, green pepper, tomato purée, salt and pepper and piri-piri. Bring to the boil and stir once. Cover and simmer over low heat for 30 mins. Remove cover and allow moisture to dry off for 5–10 mins. Fluff out rice with a fork. Garnish.

Shepherd's Pie

   2 medium carrots
   2 small turnips
   2 leeks
   2 onions
   1 lb potatoes
   2 oz vegan margarine
   ½ pt stock *or* water
   2 oz hazel nuts
   1 oz wholemeal flour
   1 tsp yeast extract

Wash and prepare the vegetables. Boil the potatoes in salt water until tender, drain, then mash them. Boil carrots, turnips and leeks in salt water until tender, then mash or liquidise them to a purée. Fry the chopped onions in ½ oz margarine.

   Roast the nuts in a slow oven (275°F, 130°C, Mk 2) for ½ hr. Rub off skin and grind or grate.

   Melt 1 oz margarine in a saucepan, add the flour and cook for 2 mins. Add the stock slowly stirring and cook for 5 mins. Add the yeast extract, nuts and ½ the onion. Add the other ½ of onion into the mashed vegetables. Grease a casserole dish. Add the mixed vegetables, then the nut mixture, top with mashed potato, patter with a fork. Top with ½ oz margarine. Bake for ½ hr at 350°F, 180°C, Mk 5.

Spaghetti with Aubergine

   1 lb wholemeal spaghetti
   1 large aubergine, chopped
   2 green peppers, chopped
   2 cloves garlic, crushed
   4 Tblsp oil
   8 oz tin tomatoes
   4 Tblsp tomato purée
   1 tsp oregano
   ½ tsp basil
   salt, pepper
   ½ pt vegetable stock

Fry aubergine, peppers, garlic in oil. Add tomatoes, purée, herbs

and seasoning. Simmer for 40 mins.
 Boil spaghetti in plenty of salt water and drain.
 Serve spaghetti covered in sauce.

Tofu Kebabs

> 2 lb firm tofu, patted dry, cut into 1 in cubes
> 3 Tblsp mustard
> 2 Tblsp olive oil
> ½ tsp sage
> 2 Tblsp vinegar
> ½ tsp rosemary
> 2 cloves garlic, chopped
> salt, pepper

In a bowl mix well mustard, vinegar, oil and spices. Add tofu cubes and sprinkle with salt and pepper. Leave to marinate in refrigerator for 3 hrs or overnight. Skewer tofu cubes and cook over open fire or under grill until brown and fragrant, baste often with marinade.
 Serve hot with vegetables.
 Serve inside pitta bread with salad.

Tomato Pilav

> 1 lb rice
> 2 lb tomatoes, skinned or 30 oz tin tomatoes
> ½ lb onions, chopped
> 3 Tblsp olive oil
> 1 clove garlic
> ½ pt water or vegetable stock
> salt, pepper
> 1 tsp sugar
> 1 bay leaf (optional)
> 1 tsp oregano (optional)

Fry onions in oil until soft. Add the whole clove of garlic, add the tomatoes and season to taste with salt, pepper and sugar. Sauté gently and squash the tomatoes with a fork. Cover the tomatoes with water or vegetable stock. Simmer gently for ½ hr. Add the oregano and bay leaf for extra flavouring if desired.

When the sauce is rich in texture, remove the clove of garlic and bay leaf. Add the rice and the same volume of water as the rice. Bring to the boil, simmer for 20 mins until rice is tender. It will be coloured and flavoured by the tomatoes.

Vegetable Curry

> 2 onions, sliced
> 1 small cauliflower, in florets
> 4 carrots, sliced
> 2 medium turnips, diced
> 4 Tblsp oil
> 1 clove garlic, crushed
> 1 Tblsp curry powder
> 1 tsp turmeric
> 1 Tblsp tomato purée
> salt, pepper
> ½ pt vegetable stock
> 5 oz tofu, creamed
> 1 Tblsp parsley, chopped

Heat oil and add onions and fry for 5 mins. Add garlic, curry powder and turmeric and cook for 2 mins. Add cauliflower, carrots, turnip, tomato purée, salt and pepper and stock. Cover and simmer for 45 mins. Stir in the tofu.

Sprinkle with parsley and serve.

Vegetable Hot-Pot

> 2 onions, sliced
> 4 large potatoes, sliced
> 4 carrots, sliced
> 4 sticks celery, sliced
> 8 oz tin baked beans
> 1 oz vegan margarine
> salt, pepper
> 1 Dsp Marmite
> 1 pt hot water
> 1 oz sesame seeds

Melt the margarine and fry the onions until golden brown.

Use a 2 pt ovenproof dish. Arrange half the sliced potatoes on the bottom. Layer the carrots, celery, onions, beans and seasoning. On the top arrange a layer of potatoes. Mix the Marmite with the hot water and pour over. Sprinkle with sesame seeds.

Cover and cook at 400°F, 200°C, Mk 6, for 1–2 hrs.

Serve with green vegetables or a salad.

Mixed Vegetable Curry

    2 Tblsp oil
    2 onions, chopped
    1 clove garlic, crushed
    1 Tblsp mustard seeds
    1 tsp coriander seeds
    1 tsp cumin seeds
    1 tsp turmeric
    1 tsp ground ginger
    ½ tsp chilli powder
    1 cooking apple, peeled and chopped
    ½ pt vegetable stock
    14 oz tin tomatoes
    1 Tblsp tomato purée
    3 potatoes, peeled and diced
    3 carrots, sliced
    8 oz cauliflower florets
    4 oz turnip, diced
    8 oz frozen peas
    1 oz raisins
    salt
    chopped nuts and coconut to garnish

Heat oil and fry onions and garlic till soft, then add all the spices and apple and stir-fry for 2 mins. Add stock, purée and vegetables, stir well and bring to the boil. Cover and place in oven 350°F, 180°C, Mk 4 for 1 hr. Stir in raisins. Season.

Serve sprinkled with nuts and coconut on a bed of rice with a salad.

Vegetable Medley

4 oz carrots
4 oz turnips
4 oz celeriac
8 oz white cabbage
1 leek
2 oz vegan margarine
1 cube miso
½ pt vegetable stock
salt, pepper
1 bay leaf
2 oz frozen peas

Peel and dice the carrots, turnips and celeriac. Chop the cabbage. Wash and slice the leek. Melt the margarine in a saucepan. Fry the leek for 2 mins, add diced vegetables and sauté, add cabbage. Sprinkle with miso. Add vegetable stock and bring to the boil. Add seasoning and bay leaf, cover and simmer for 30 mins. Add the peas and simmer uncovered for 5 mins. Remove bay leaf and pile into serving dish.

Vegetable Stew

3 onions, chopped
4 Tblsp oil
1½ lb root vegetables, mixed
2 sticks celery, sliced
2 cloves garlic, crushed
4 tomatoes, skinned and chopped
6 oz red lentils
1½ pt vegetable stock
2 tsp ground coriander
2 tsp ground cumin
1 Tblsp lemon juice
salt, pepper

Fry half the onion in half the oil for 5 mins. Add the rest of the vegetables and lentils. Fry for 5 mins, stirring all the time. Add the stock, simmer gently uncovered until the lentils and vegetables are tender, about 30 mins. Fry the rest of the onion, coriander and cumin in the remaining oil for 10 mins. Add to

lentil mixture along with lemon juice and seasoning.
Serve with baked potatoes or cooked rice.
(This dish freezes well.)

Vegetable Platter

1 ½ lb carrots
1 ½ lb small Brussels sprouts
1 lb small onions
1 lb courgettes
½ lb button mushrooms
2 cauliflower florets
2 tsp sugar
1 tsp chopped mint
5 oz vegan margarine
salt, pepper
juice of ½ lemon
1 Dsp chopped parsley

Carrots

Young ones leave whole; otherwise quarter. Cover with cold water, add ½ tsp salt, 1 tsp sugar and ½ oz margarine. Cook until tender. Remove lid and allow water to evaporate. Sprinkle with 1 tsp mint.

Brussels Sprouts

Boil in salt water for 8 mins until tender.
Drain and toss in ½ oz margarine.

Onions

Blanch and remove skins. Cook slowly in a covered pan with ½ oz margarine and 1 tsp sugar until brown and sticky, about 8 mins.

Courgettes

Slice thickly and blanch for 1 min in boiling water. Drain. Cook with ½ oz margarine in covered pan for 8 mins until tender.

Mushrooms

Cook quickly in 1 oz margarine with a squeeze of lemon juice.
Drain on absorbent paper.

Cauliflower

Cook florets in boiling water for 8 mins. Drain. Turn in ½ oz
melted margarine.

Arrange vegetables in rows on a large hot serving dish.

Melt 1½ oz margarine in a pan until nut-brown. Add lemon
juice, salt and pepper and chopped parsley. Pour this mixture
hot over all the vegetables.

Mixed Spring Vegetable Stew   *Serves 6*

    ½ lb young carrots
    2 heads lettuce
    ½ lb spinach
    1 medium cucumber
    2 heads spring greens
    ½ lb French beans
    1 tsp ground ginger *or* 2 1-in slices of root ginger
    3 Tblsp vegetable oil
    3 stalks spring onions to garnish
    2 cloves garlic, crushed
    ¾ lb bean sprouts
    4 tomatoes, quartered
    2 Tblsp vegetable fat
    1½ pt vegetable stock
    2 Tblsp yeast extract
    salt, pepper
    2 tsp sesame oil

Wash and prepare all the vegetables. Cut the carrots diagonally
into 1-inch sections. Cut lettuce, spinach, cucumber and spring
greens into 1-inch slices. Cut French beans in half. Cut spring
onions into ½-inch sections. Crush ginger.

Heat oil in a large saucepan. Add garlic, ginger and carrots.
Stir-fry for 3 mins over medium heat. Add spring greens and
beans and stir for 2 mins at a low heat, then simmer for 5 mins.
Add all other vegetables (except the spring onions), fat, stock,
yeast extract and seasoning. Bring to the boil and simmer for 15

mins. Sprinkle with spring onion stalks and sesame oil.

Serve with warm wholemeal bread.

Variation

2 Tblsp of curry powder may be added into the initial frying with the garlic. Stir-fry for 2 mins extra to give the curry a chance to develop.

Vegetable Crumble   *

6½ oz whole wheat flour
4 oz vegan margarine
2 Tblsp sesame seeds
2 onions, sliced
4 carrots, diced
4 sticks celery, chopped
1 Tblsp yeast extract
¾ pt boiling water
½ lb cabbage, shredded
8 oz tomatoes, skinned and sliced
4 oz mushrooms, sliced
salt, pepper

Sift 5 oz of flour into a mixing bowl. Rub in ½ margarine. Stir in sesame seeds. Set aside.

Melt remaining margarine in a large frying pan and cook onions, carrot and celery for 10 mins until soft. Stir in remaining flour and cook for 2 mins.

Dissolve yeast extract in boiling water and add to pan. Cook, stirring until thickened, then add remaining vegetables and seasoning.

Pour into casserole dish and sprinkle crumble over the top.

Place in oven (350°F, 180°C, Mk 4) and cook for 1 hr until golden.

When offered seconds of this dish a guest asked for – 'A nice meaty spoonful from the middle'!

Gravies and Sauces

Almond Sauce

> 2 oz ground almonds
> 1 pt vegetable stock
> salt, pepper
> 1 clove garlic, crushed
> 2 Tblsp chopped parsley (reserve a little to garnish)
> ½ tsp sugar
> juice of 1 lemon
> pinch of turmeric

Mix the almonds and cold stock together in a saucepan. Bring to the boil and season. Add all the ingredients together and simmer gently stirring occasionally for 20 mins, until the mixture thickens and becomes flavoursome.

Serve garnished with reserved parsley. This is a good accompaniment for rice dishes.

Basic Gravy

The thickness of the gravy depends upon the amount of flour used. For a thin gravy use no flour or very little. For a thick gravy use 1 Tblsp flour to ½ pint stock.

> 2 Tblsp vegetable oil
> 1 Tblsp flour *or* less
> ½ pt vegetable stock
> 1 Tblsp yeast extract
> salt, pepper

Heat the oil and stir in the flour and blend thoroughly, cooking until the flour browns. Gradually blend in the hot stock and yeast extract. Bring the gravy to the boil and simmer for 2–3 mins. Season.

Bisto Gravy Powder could also be used to brown the gravy.

Dal

8 oz red lentils
1½ pt water
1 bay leaf
2 in cinnamon stick
4 cardamoms, split
2 tsp ground coriander
2 tsp ground cumin
4 Tblsp oil
2 onions, chopped
2 cloves garlic, crushed
1 Tblsp lemon juice
salt, pepper

Put lentils, water, bay leaf and cinnamon stick into a saucepan. Cook gently until lentils are tender, 20 mins. Fry spices in oil for 2 mins, then add onions and garlic and fry for 10 mins until tender. Add this mixture including the oil to the cooked lentils, stir in lemon juice and seasoning.

Serve poured over cooked root vegetables.

Serve as a side dish to curries.

(It freezes well.)

Onion Gravy

1 lb onions
3 oz vegan margarine
pinch brown sugar
1 Tblsp flour
1 tsp vinegar
salt, pepper
¼ pt vegetable stock

Thinly slice the onions and fry in 2 oz of margarine over a low heat for 20 mins until they are soft and golden brown. Turn them frequently to prevent them sticking and a little brown sugar may be added to help them brown more quickly.

Blend 1 oz margarine with the flour and add in knobs to the hot onions. Stir until melted and blended, then slowly add the hot stock. Simmer gently and stir in the vinegar and seasoning.

Okra and Tomato Gravy

    4 oz okra
    4 tomatoes
    ½ pt vegetable stock
    1 Dsp flour
    1 Tbsp soya sauce
    pinch of black pepper

Slice the okra and tomatoes and boil together gently in a little of the stock, until the okra is very soft and pulpy.

Cream the flour in a little cold stock and add to the okra mixture stirring continuously. Stir in the soya sauce, black pepper and remaining stock and bring back to the boil, stirring until the sauce thickens.

Tahini with Walnuts

    ¼ lb walnuts
    2 cloves garlic
    salt
    4 Tblsp tahini paste
    juice of 2 lemons
    4 Tblsp chopped parsley

Place all the ingredients in an electric blender, or use a mortar. Do not over-blend the walnuts or they lose their rough texture. A little water may be needed.

Serve with steamed runner beans or cauliflower florets.

Tomato Sauce

    14 oz tin tomatoes
    1 Dsp dried basil
    1 Dsp sugar

Place all the ingredients in an electric blender and liquidise.

This sauce is very colourful and can be used to add colour to a meal.

This sauce may be served either chilled or hot, but do not allow to boil.

Savoury Spreads

Chutney Spread

    4 oz vegan margarine
    4 oz chutney – apple, tomato
    ½ tsp lemon juice

Cream ingredients.

Devilled Mustard Spread

    4 oz vegan margarine
    ½ tsp curry powder
    ¼ tsp grated lemon rind
    2 tsp prepared mustard
    1 Tblsp lemon juice

Cream ingredients.

Garlic Spread

    2 oz vegan margarine
    salt, pepper
    2 cloves garlic, crushed

Cream ingredients.

Herb Spread – Recipe 1

    4 oz vegan margarine
    1 Tblsp chopped chives
    ½ tsp chopped tarragon
    ½ tsp rosemary

Cream ingredients.

Herb Spread – Recipe 2

4 oz vegan margarine
juice of ¼ lemon
2 Tblsp mixed herbs
black pepper

Cream ingredients.

Maître d'Hôtel Spread

4 oz vegan margarine
1 tsp lemon juice
1 Tblsp chopped parsley
salt, pepper

Cream ingredients.
Serve with nut-made sausages, burgers, and cutlets.
Serve on biscuits, bread or toast.

Salads

Avocado and Apple Salad

2 avocados
2 eating apples
1 bunch of watercress
½ cup salted peanuts

Dressing:
½ cup oil
3 Tblsp lemon juice
1 tsp mustard
1 tsp sugar
1 clove garlic, crushed
salt, pepper

Mix together all the ingredients for the dressing and beat well.

Cut the avocados in half and remove the stone. Remove the flesh without damaging the skins, which are placed on one side. Chop the flesh. Core the apple, chop and place in dressing. Reserve 4 sprigs of watercress and chop the remainder. Chop the peanuts. Toss all in the dressing.

Pile back in the avocado shells and garnish with watercress.

Basic Green Salad

1 lettuce, any type
3 Tblsp oil
1 Tblsp vinegar
salt, pepper
1 tsp mixed herbs
1 small onion, finely chopped

In a salad bowl whisk together oil, vinegar, salt and pepper until the mixture becomes thick and creamy. Then mix in the herbs and onion.

Wash and dry the lettuce and tear it into bite-size pieces. Add to the dressing and toss.

Serve immediately.

A Green Salad may be used as the base for a Mixed Salad. Chop up and add vegetables of choice: red or green peppers, mushrooms, tomatoes, cucumber, mustard and cress, radishes. (See also p.70.)

Bean and Tomato Salad

8 oz runner beans, sliced
8 oz tomatoes, sliced
1 small onion, chopped
2 Tblsp Salad Dressing (p.77)
salt
parsley, chopped to garnish

Cook beans in boiling water until tender. Drain and refresh under cold water, drain and leave to cool.

Place beans, tomatoes and onion in salad bowl. Pour over dressing, season and toss. Chill well. Garnish with parsley.

Beetroot Salad

2 lb cooked beetroot, sliced
1 large onion, sliced
8 Tblsp vinegar
8 Tblsp water
1 Dsp sugar
1 bay leaf
4 peppercorns
2 whole cloves
½ tsp salt
½ tsp caraway seeds

Place sliced beetroot and onion rings in a deep glass dish.

Place remaining ingredients in a saucepan and bring to the boil. When boiling point is just reached, pour marinade over beetroot and onions. Leave to cool and refrigerate.

This salad will keep in the refrigerator for a week if tightly covered.

Brown Rice Salad

>8 oz brown rice
>2 spring onions
>2 stalks celery
>1 red pepper, sliced
>2 oz dates, chopped
>1 oz blanched almonds, toasted
>1 Tblsp sunflower seeds
>2 Tblsp oil
>1 Tblsp apple juice, unsweetened
>2 Tblsp cider vinegar
>2 tsp bran
>1 tsp curry powder
>1 clove garlic, crushed
>salt, pepper

Cook rice in salt water for 45 mins, drain.

Toss together rice, vegetables, dates, almonds and sunflower seeds.

Mix oil, apple juice, vinegar, bran, curry powder, garlic and seasoning.

Just before serving pour dressing over salad and toss.

Carrot Salad

>4 large carrots
>2 oranges
>salt, pepper
>1 Tblsp oil
>sprig of watercress

Peel then grate carrots. Remove zest from both oranges, then squeeze the juice from one. Beat orange zest, salt, pepper and oil. Pour dressing over grated carrot, cover and chill. Segment other orange.

Serve salad decorated with orange segments and garnished with watercress.

Beetroot Relish

>   2 large cooked beetroots
>   2 cooking apples
>   4 Tblsp French Dressing with garlic (p.77)

Dice beetroot, peel, quarter and core apple and dice. Mix together, moisten with French Dressing.

This recipe is a great favourite with the children. It is delicious, refreshing and colourful. It goes well at a party.

Celery Salad

>   1 large head celery
>   8 oz cooked green peas
>   6 spring onions, chopped
>   sprig of watercress
>   ½ tsp salt, ¼ tsp pepper
>   1 tsp prepared mustard
>   1 lemon, juice and grated rind
>   6 Tblsp oil

Clean and trim celery, slice obliquely in 1-inch lengths. Mix together dressing ingredients and beat in oil slowly.

Toss the salad and dressing and garnish with watercress.

Chinese Leaves and Avocado Salad

>   1 small head Chinese leaves
>   1 small green pepper
>   2 stalks of celery
>   ½ small red cabbage
>   2 tomatoes
>   1 large avocado
>   2 oz raisins
>   ¼ pt Tofu Dressing (p.78)
>   2 oz flaked almonds, toasted
>   squeeze of lemon

Chop Chinese leaves, pepper, celery and red cabbage. Quarter tomatoes. Peel avocado, remove stone and slice flesh.

Mix all prepared ingredients together in a bowl. Keep some

avocado on one side for garnish. Add raisins and stir in dressing. Sprinkle nuts over the top.

Garnish with reserved avocado slices, dipped in lemon juice.

Coleslaw

> 1 small white cabbage
> 1 small green pepper, sliced
> 1 tsp celery salt
> salt, pepper
> ½ tsp sugar
> 1 Tblsp vinegar
> 1 Tblsp oil
> chopped chives *or* parsley

Quarter cabbage and shred finely. Place in a bowl with the sliced pepper.

Place all the ingredients in a screw-top jar and shake vigorously. Pour this mixture over the cabbage. Toss well. Garnish with chives or parsley.

Croutons with Salad

> 2 large slices bread (pref. stale), trimmed
> oil for frying
> 1 clove garlic
> 1 lettuce
> ½ cucumber
> 4 Tblsp French Dressing (p.77)
> 4 spring onions
> 1 Tblsp chopped parsley

Dice bread and fry until golden. Drain. Rub salad bowl with garlic. Shred lettuce and slice cucumber and spring onions.

Toss all ingredients in French Dressing and serve.

Cucumber Salad

> 1 cucumber
> 2 Tblsp oil
> 2 Tblsp vinegar
> 1 small onion *or* spring onions, finely chopped
> salt, pepper
> ¼ tsp dried dill

Halve the cucumber, lengthwise, and peel from the centre to the tip. Slice into thin even slices. Mix together dressing and add cucumber. Toss and serve chilled.

This salad is very juicy and children love the juice. If less juice is required sprinkle cucumber slices with salt and leave to drain for 30 mins.

Cucumber and Potato Salad

> 2 medium cucumbers
> 8 oz cooked new potatoes
> 1½ oz flour
> salt, pepper
> 2 oz vegan margarine
> 1 Tblsp chopped parsley
> lemon slices

Peel and cut cucumbers into ½ inch cubes. Cube potatoes. Season flour with salt and pepper. Toss the cucumber and potato in the flour. Fry the vegetables in the heated margarine until brown, about 15 mins. Add parsley.

Serve hot with lemon.

Leek Salad

> 2 lb leeks
> ¼ pt French Dressing (p77)
> chopped parsley
> seasoning

Wash and boil leeks in salt water until tender. Drain.

Place in shallow dish. Pour over dressing and leave for 12

hours turning leeks occasionally.

Before serving remove from dressing and roll in seasoning and parsley.

Lentil Salad

> ½ lb brown lentils, soaked overnight
> salt
> ¼ pt Vegetable Dressing (p.79)
> 3 Tblsp chopped parsley

Drain lentils and boil them in fresh water until nearly tender, about 1 hr. Add salt towards the end of cooking. Drain. Place in a serving dish. Pour over dressing and stir in parsley.

Variation

The lentils may be boiled until very soft. Drain and purée by mashing or in a blender with the dressing.

Mushroom and Spinach Salad

> 4 oz button mushrooms, sliced
> 4 Tblsp French Dressing (p.77)
> 4 oz spinach

Put mushrooms in a salad bowl with 2 Tblsp dressing and stir until well coated. Leave to soak for 1 hr. Discard thick centre stalk from spinach. Wash and dry leaves. Slice them finely and mix with mushrooms. Add remainder of the dressing if required.

Orange Salad

> 3 oranges
> ½ tsp ground cinnamon

Peel and remove all the bitter white pith. Slice very thinly. Arrange on a plate. Dust lightly with ground cinnamon.

Mixed Salad

> 1 lb carrots
> 1 lb white cabbage
> 1 green pepper
> 1 bunch of spring onions
> 1 bunch of radishes
> 4 tomatoes
> ½ pt French Dressing (p.77)

Shred cabbage and slice carrots thinly. Chop green pepper and onions, slice radishes and dice tomatoes. Toss all in the dressing. Place in the refrigerator for 1 hr to blend flavours.

Mixed Salad with Orange

> 2 tomatoes
> 2 small cucumbers
> 6 olives
> 1 large raw carrot, peeled
> 1 raw beetroot, peeled
> 2 Tblsp Tahini Salad Dressing (p.77)
> 2 avocado pears, peeled and stoned
> 2 firm potatoes, boiled
> 1 large mild onion
> 1 sweet pepper
> 1 orange, segmented

Chop all the ingredients or cut them into small dice. Mix them together in a bowl. Dress with Tahini Salad Dressing.

Orange and Avocado Pear Salad

> 2 oranges
> 1 avocado pear
> salt, pepper
> 1 Tblsp lemon juice
> 3 Tblsp olive oil
> pinch of sugar

Peel and segment the oranges and cut into medium-sized pieces. Cut avocado into pieces and mix together. Season with dressing.

Orange and Lettuce Salad

>2 oranges
>French Dressing (p.77)
>1 crisp lettuce

Peel and thinly cut the oranges into rings. Arrange them on the crisp lettuce. Serve with French Dressing.

Orange and Pineapple Salad

>2 oranges
>1 crisp lettuce
>1 small pineapple

Peel, core and dice the pineapple. Peel and cut the oranges into rings. Arrange on a bed of crisp lettuce.

Orange and Radish Salad

>2 oranges
>1 bunch of radishes
>salt
>1 Tblsp lemon juice

Peel oranges, slice and cut into pieces. Thinly slice radishes. Mix together and season with salt and lemon juice.

Orange and Tomato Salad

>2 oranges
>4 medium tomatoes
>1 crisp lettuce *or* watercress
>mint, chopped
>French Dressing (p.77)

This is very colourful. The oranges and tomatoes should both be cut into either rings or segments. On a bed of lettuce or watercress alternate layers of oranges and tomatoes. Sprinkle with mint.

Serve with French Dressing.

Potato Salad

    1½ lb new potatoes
    salt
    4 Tblsp olive oil
    3 Tblsp lemon juice
    2 cloves garlic, crushed
    salt, pepper
    3 Tblsp chopped parsley
    3 Tblsp chopped spring onions

Wash potatoes. Boil in salt water until just tender. Drain and allow to cool. Peel potatoes and cut into cubes. Mix the dressing well. Pour over potatoes, sprinkle with parsley and onions and toss well. Season with salt and pepper to taste.

It will keep well in an airtight container in the refrigerator for one week.

Tabbouleh (Cracked Wheat Salad)   *serves 6*

    8 oz fine cracked wheat (bulgur)
    ½ pt water
    3 Tblsp chopped spring onions, *or* 1 onion
    4 tomatoes, skinned, deseeded and chopped
    salt, pepper
    4 Tblsp olive oil
    4 Tblsp lemon juice
    1½ cups chopped parsley
    3 Tblsp chopped mint *or* 2 Tblsp dried mint
    cooked vine leaves *or* lettuce *or* raw tender cabbage leaves
    1 tsp paprika
    black olives to garnish

Soak the wheat in the water for 1 hr to allow the grain to swell. Drain and squeeze out as much water as possible with your hands. Spread out to dry on a cloth. Mix the wheat, chopped onion and tomato together. Season to taste. Beat together the olive oil and lemon juice, add the parsley and mint and mix well. Pour over the wheat mixture and stir well.

The salad should be distinctly lemony.

To serve, line individual plates with leaves of choice and place portions of salad on each. Decorate with a sprinkle of paprika and black olives.

Alternatively line a large serving dish with the leaves, pile wheat mixture into a pyramid on top and decorate.

Red Cabbage and Apple Salad

> 1 lb red cabbage
> 1 green eating apple, skinned
> 1 celery heart
> 1 bunch of watercress
> ½ tsp salt, ¼ tsp pepper
> ½ tsp dry mustard
> pinch of sugar
> 1 Tblsp lemon juice
> 2 Tblsp oil

Shred cabbage finely, core and slice apple evenly. Slice celery heart finely and chop up watercress and reserve 4 sprigs for garnish.

Stir salt, pepper, mustard and sugar into lemon juice and beat in the oil. Toss salad in the dressing. Divide into 4 small bowls and garnish with watercress.

Red Coleslaw with Celery

> 1 small red cabbage
> ½ head celery
> 3 oranges
> 2 oz walnut halves
> salt, pepper
> ½ tsp mustard
> 1 Tblsp oil

Finely shred the cabbage. Chop the celery into short lengths. Peel 2 oranges and divide into segments, removing pith and membrane. Mix all together with walnuts.

Squeeze the juice from the third orange. Season the juice with salt, pepper and mustard and beat in the oil. Pour over the salad and toss.

Spanish Salad

> 1 onion, thinly sliced
> 1 orange, peeled
> salt, pepper
> 4 Tblsp oil
> 4 Tblsp vinegar
> 1 lettuce

Separate the onion slices into rings and place in the bowl. Break the orange into segments removing membrane and pips.

Beat together the dressing and pour over, leaving to marinate for 1 hr.

Wash and dry the lettuce and tear into pieces. Toss in marinade just before serving.

Spinach Salad

> 6 raw spinach leaves
> 1 small cucumber
> salt, pepper
> 2 Tblsp vinegar
> 4 Tblsp oil
> ½ tsp dry mustard

Wash spinach and discard stems. Dry leaves and tear into pieces. Peel cucumber and cut into cubes. Sprinkle with salt and leave for 1 hr to drain. Rinse. Beat together dressing ingredients. Pour over spinach and cucumber and toss.

Sweet Pepper Salad

> 3 sweet green peppers
> 2 Tblsp Salad Dressing (p.77)
> 1 Tblsp parsley, chopped

Cut peppers in half and remove seeds. Grill the peppers under a low flame until the skins blister, and the flesh becomes soft. Skin them and cut them into long strips. Put the peppers in a serving bowl and pour over the Salad Dressing including the parsley.

Tomato Salad

> 1½ lb firm tomatoes, sliced
> 1 small mild onion *or* 3 spring onions, chopped
> 2 Tblsp parsley, chopped
> ½ tsp ground cumin
> Salad Dressing (p.77)

Mix the tomatoes, onions, parsley and cumin in a bowl.
Pour over the salad dressing and toss well.

Alternative:

Arrange the tomato slices overlapping in rows on a serving dish.
Pour over the Salad Dressing and sprinkle with onions, parsley
and cumin.

Tomato and Onion Salad

> 1 lb ripe tomatoes, sliced
> 1 onion, thinly sliced
> 3 Tblsp oil
> 1 Tblsp vinegar
> salt, pepper
> 1 tsp dried basil

Separate the onion rings. Place layers of onions and tomato
slices in a dish. Beat the dressing ingredients together well and
pour over.
Serve chilled.

Toureto (Cucumber and Bread Salad)

> 5 slices wholemeal bread (without crusts)
> 1 large cucumber, peeled and chopped
> 2 cloves garlic, crushed
> 4 Tblsp olive oil
> juice of ½ lemon
> salt, pepper
> 1 tsp paprika mixed with 1 Tblsp olive oil to garnish

Soak bread in water and squeeze dry. Mix with other ingredients. Purée to a smooth cream. Place in a serving dish and chill.
Serve garnished with olive oil and paprika.

Vegetable Salad

> 2 potatoes
> 1 beetroot
> 2 courgettes
> ¼ lb runner beans
> 1 small cauliflower
> salt
> Salad Dressing (p.77)

Keep all the vegetables separate. Peel potatoes, scrub beetroot and courgettes, string and wash runner beans and wash cauliflower.

Boil separately in salt water or steam. Drain.

Cube potatoes, peel beetroot and dice, slice courgettes into rounds, slice runner beans lengthways or into 2-inch lengths, separate cauliflower into florets.

Arrange vegetables in separate groups on serving dish and sprinkle with Salad Dressing. The vegetables used may be varied.

Walnut Salad

> 2 oz walnut halves
> 1 oz seedless raisins
> 2 Tblsp French Dressing (p.77)
> 2 slices of onion
> 1 large tomato
> 1 lb white cabbage

Soak raisins in dressing for 2 hrs until plump. Break onion slices into rings. Slice tomato. Shred cabbage into a bowl. Add walnuts, raisins and dressing and toss.

Decorate with onion and tomato.

When Salad Vegetables are Scarce

When salad vegetables are scarce and expensive, use thinly sliced cabbage, red or white; tiny raw cauliflower florets; crisp shredded Brussels sprouts; with nuts and citrus fruit to garnish.

Salad Dressings and Sauces

Salad Dressing

> 1 Tblsp lemon *or* vinegar
> 3 Tblsp olive oil
> 1 clove garlic, crushed
> salt, black pepper

Mix well and pour over salad just before serving.

Additional flavourings are chopped parsley, fresh or dried mint, dill, and fresh coriander.

French Dressing

> 4 Tblsp olive oil
> 1 tsp dried mustard
> 2 Tblsp vinegar
> salt, black pepper

Mix well and pour over salad just before serving.

Additional flavourings are 1 clove garlic, crushed, 1 Tblsp chopped chives, 1 Dsp tomato purée, 1 Dsp grated onion, or a pinch of paprika.

Tahini Salad Dressing

> ¼ pt tahini paste
> 2 cloves garlic
> salt
> ¼ pt lemon juice
> cold water
> ½ tsp ground cumin
> 2 Tblsp finely chopped parsley

Crush the garlic with the salt, mix well with a little lemon juice in a large bowl. Add tahini paste and mix well. Add remaining lemon juice and enough cold water to achieve a thick creamy paste. Beat well. Add cumin. Taste and adjust seasoning and lemon juice until the flavour is fairly strong and tart. Garnish with parsley.

Tarator Sauce

> 2 slices wholemeal bread (without crusts)
> ¼ lb walnuts and hazelnuts, ground
> ¼ pt olive oil
> 4 Tblsp vinegar
> 2 cloves garlic, crushed
> salt, pepper

Dip the bread in water and squeeze dry. Crumble it and add the ground nuts. Gradually add the oil, beating constantly. Stir in the vinegar and garlic and season to taste. The sauce should be smooth and creamy.

Serve separately in a bowl.

Serve with the plainer vegetable salads.

Tofu Dressing

> 6 oz tofu
> 2 Tblsp cider vinegar
> 2 Tblsp vegetable oil
> 1 Tblsp soya sauce or salt and pepper

Drain and dice the tofu and beat it with the other ingredients until it is smooth and creamy.

Tofu Dressing will keep for a week sealed in the refrigerator.

Vegan Salad Dressing

> 2 Tblsp lemon juice
> 2 Tblsp vegetable oil
> 2 Tblsp concentrated soya milk

Whisk together lemon juice and oil and stir in enough concentrated soya milk to give a creamy consistency.

Vegetable Salad Dressing

> 6 Tblsp olive oil *or* vegetable oil
> ½ tsp ground coriander *or* cumin
> 2 cloves garlic, crushed
> juice of 2 lemons
> black pepper

Mix all ingredients together well.

Watercress Dressing

> 1 bunch watercress
> 2 Tblsp lemon juice
> 1 Tblsp vinegar
> 1 tsp dried tarragon
> 5 Tblsp olive oil
> salt, pepper

Chop the watercress finely and set aside. Mix all the other ingredients together and blend well. Stir in the watercress.
  Use over green salads.

Vegetables

For years vegetables have been cleaned, put in a large pan with plenty of water and cooked slowly to death.

At last their importance is being realized. They are a rich source of nutrition. They look good, taste good and can be cooked in a variety of methods. Freshness is important. Many vegetables can be eaten raw. It is important to cook vegetables for as short a time as possible to keep their goodness.

Whether vegetables are boiled or steamed, the saucepan lid should always be kept on.

It is not necessary to add bicarbonate of soda.

The Chinese method of cooking vegetables by stir-frying in a little vegetable oil for 2–5 mins, then adding vegetable stock and simmering for 5–10 mins, preserves nearly all the goodness.

Vegetable Stock

Generally the water that vegetables have been cooked in makes a good stock, especially: spinach, broccoli, courgettes, marrow, and potato water. Or: wash the vegetables carefully before trimming and peeling. Boil up these trimmings and peelings to make a basic stock. Alternatively use a vegetable stock cube.

Vegetable stock will freeze and keep up to 3 months.

Stuffed Vegetables

Almost any vegetable can be stuffed.

Stuffing a vegetable is decorative but can be very time-consuming. Remember, as Shirley Conran said, 'Life is too short to stuff a mushroom'.

Fillings for Stuffed Vegetables
Stuffs about 2 lb of vegetables

> 6 oz rice, cooked
> 1 Tblsp parsley, chopped
> 1 onion, chopped
> ½ tsp ground cinnamon
> 6 oz tomatoes, skinned and chopped
> salt, black pepper

Mix all ingredients together in a bowl.
   Pack tightly into the vegetable to be baked.

Variation:

> 2 tsp chopped dill *or* mint
> 2 oz chick peas, cooked
> 4 oz rice, cooked
> ¼ tsp ground allspice
> 1 onion, chopped
> 1 Tblsp parsley, chopped
> 6 oz tomatoes, skinned, chopped

Prepare as above.

To Make Vegetables Extra Special

> 1 Tblsp lemon juice
> pinch oregano
> ½ clove garlic, chopped
> salt, pepper
> 4 oz vegan margarine

Mix all ingredients into the margarine.
   Serve with any vegetable.

Carrots

Add the juice of 1 orange while boiling, glaze with warmed syrup and melted vegan margarine.

Cauliflower

After boiling break into florets. Heat 1 Tblsp vegan margarine with 1 Tblsp olive oil, add juice of 1 lemon and salt and pepper. Roll cauliflower in this over low heat until lemon juice is absorbed.

Green Beans

Add almonds sautéed in vegan margarine.

Aubergine Fried

> 4 medium aubergines
> salt, black pepper
> 2 Tblsp oil

Cut the aubergine in ½ lengthwise, make several ½-in slashes in the sides. Sprinkle all over with salt and leave for 30 mins. Wash and dry. Sprinkle with black pepper. Fry aubergine halves in hot oil gently for 8 mins, until golden brown.

Bean Sprouts Stir-Fried

> 1 lb fresh bean sprouts
> 3 Tblsp oil
> 2 cloves garlic, crushed
> 2 slices root ginger, shredded
> sea salt, pepper
> 1½ Tblsp soya sauce
> 3 spring onions, cut into 2-inch pieces
> 1½ tsp sesame seed oil

Speed is essential. Heat oil until hot, add garlic and ginger and stir-fry for a few seconds. Add bean sprouts, season to taste. Turn bean sprouts quickly so they become evenly coated with oil. Add soya sauce and spring onions. Stir-fry over high heat for 2 mins.

Sprinkle with sesame oil and serve immediately.

Beetroot with Orange and Lemon

2 lb beetroot
2 Tblsp lemon juice
½ tsp grated lemon zest
4 Tblsp orange juice
½ tsp grated orange zest
1 Tblsp vinegar
1 Tblsp sugar
1 Tblsp cornflour
salt, pepper
2 oz vegan margarine

Cook beetroot in boiling water until tender (50 mins). Peel. Cut into ½-inch dice. Combine lemon juice, orange juice, vinegar, sugar and cornflour. Bring to the boil and cook over medium heat until sauce is thick and clear. Remove from heat. Add diced beetroot, salt, pepper and margarine. Heat through.

Pour into serving dish and garnish with grated orange and lemon zest.

Brussels Sprouts and Celery

1 lb Brussels sprouts
1 stick celery
1 oz vegan margarine
1 onion, chopped
1 oz wholemeal flour
¾ pt soya milk
½ oz melted vegan margarine
2 Tblsp breadcrumbs

Boil sprouts in salt water for 8 mins. Blanch celery in boiling water for 1 min and chop. Melt margarine, add onion and celery and cook for a few mins until soft.

Stir in flour then blend in soya milk. Add the sprouts and turn into an ovenproof dish. Sprinkle with melted margarine and breadcrumbs. Brown in a hot oven (400°F, 200°C, Mk 6) for 10 mins.

Brussels Sprouts with Chestnuts

> 1½ lb Brussels sprouts
> 1 lb chestnuts
> 1 oz vegan margarine
> ¾ pt vegetable stock
> salt, pepper

Blanch and skin chestnuts. Boil and drain sprouts. Put the chestnuts in a pan with ½ the margarine and stock. Cover and cook until soft and stock absorbed. Put sprouts in frying pan with remaining margarine and seasoning, shake gently until coated. Mix in chestnuts.

Serve.

Cabbage Braised

> 1 white cabbage
> 1 large onion
> 1 oz vegan margarine
> 1 cooking apple, peeled and sliced
> salt, pepper
> 2 Tblsp vegetable stock

Shred cabbage finely. Slice onion. Melt margarine and fry onion until soft. Add cabbage and apple. Season. Stir well and pour in the stock. Cover with greaseproof paper and lid. Cook for 45 mins on bottom shelf of oven (325°F, 160°C, Mk 3).

Carrots Glacés

> 4 large carrots
> salt
> 2 oz vegan margarine
> 2 oz syrup
> 1 Tblsp mustard
> 1 Tblsp chopped almonds

Peel and cut carrots into 1-inch slices. Cook in boiling salt water for 10 mins until tender. Melt margarine, syrup and mustard together and cook over low heat for 3 mins until well blended. Drain carrots. Pour the sauce over carrots and sprinkle with chopped almonds.

Cauliflower with Almonds

> 1 large cauliflower
> 1½ oz almonds
> 4 Tblsp breadcrumbs
> 1½ oz vegan margarine
> ½ clove garlic, chopped
> salt, pepper

Break cauliflower into large florets. Cook in boiling water until tender (15 mins). Blanch and shred almonds and soak in boiling water.

Drain cauliflower. Grease a large basin and arrange cauliflower in it. Cover with a small plate and press down lightly. Drain almonds, dry well and mix with breadcrumbs.

Heat margarine, add garlic and almond mixture. Stir until brown. Season.

Turn out moulded cauliflower on to a warm serving dish and spoon over almond and breadcrumb mixture.

Serve with Tomato Sauce (p.60).

Corn-on-the-Cob Roasted

> 4 sweetcorn cobs
> ½ tsp marjoram
> ½ tsp rosemary
> salt
> 2 oz vegan margarine
> 8 large cabbage leaves

Mix the herbs, sprinkling of salt and margarine together. Spread over corn cobs. Place 4 cabbage leaves on tinfoil. Arrange corn cobs on cabbage leaves and cover with remaining 4 leaves. Seal tinfoil tightly.

Bake in hot oven (425°F, 220°C, Mk 7) for 25–30 mins. Discard cabbage leaves and serve.

Courgettes Buttered

>8 courgettes
>1½ oz vegan margarine
>1 Tblsp water
>salt, pepper
>½ Tblsp chopped parsley
>½ Tblsp mixed herbs, fresh, chopped

Wipe and trim courgettes. Place in pan with margarine and water. Add seasoning and cover with lid. Cook slowly for 15 mins until tender.

Sprinkle with parsley and herbs and serve.

Cucumber and Carrots

>1 large cucumber, peeled
>½ lb new carrots, peeled
>½ oz vegan margarine
>1 tsp sugar
>salt, pepper
>1 Dsp chopped parsley

Cut the cucumber in half lengthways and then into ½-inch slices. Blanch in boiling water for 1 min. Drain. Quarter carrots and put in a pan with margarine, sugar, salt and enough water to cover. Cook with lid on for 10 mins until tender. Remove lid and cook until water evaporates. Add cucumber, parsley and seasoning to taste. Toss vegetables carefully until they are all coated.

Cucumber Hot

>1 large cucumber
>1 oz vegan margarine
>1 Tblsp chopped fresh herbs, parsley, mint, thyme

Dice the unpeeled cucumber. Sprinkle with salt and leave for 1 hr. Pour off excess fluid. Heat margarine and sauté cucumber for 2 mins over low heat. Sprinkle on herbs.

Serve hot.

(This freezes well.)

Sweet and Sour Leeks

> 1 lb leeks
> 1 clove garlic, crushed
> 1 Dsp sugar
> 2 Tblsp vegetable oil
> juice of 1 lemon

Carefully wash the leeks. Cut into long slices.

Fry the garlic and sugar in hot oil until the sugar starts to caramelise. Add the leeks and turn them over moderate heat. Sprinkle with lemon juice. Cover, stew gently over low heat until tender.

Serve hot or cold.

Marrow Stuffed with Sweetcorn

> 1 large marrow
> 2 oz vegan margarine
> 1 onion, chopped
> 2 tomatoes, chopped
> 1 oz wholemeal flour
> 1 tin sweetcorn
> 2 Tblsp tomato purée
> 1 Tblsp soya sauce
> 1 tsp mixed herbs
> salt, pepper

Peel and cut marrow in half lengthwise. Remove centre, being careful not to puncture ends of marrow. Place in boiling water for 3 mins, remove and drain. Melt margarine and fry onions and tomatoes until soft. Add wholemeal flour and stir for 2 mins. Add drained juice from sweetcorn made up to ¼ pint. Stir until sauce thickens. Add tomato purée and soya sauce and sweetcorn. Mix in herbs and seasoning.

Place a large sheet of tinfoil on a baking tray. Place marrow halves upright on tinfoil. Fill the hollow centres of marrow with sweetcorn mixture. Seal over with tinfoil. Bake in oven (350°F, 180°C, Mk 4) for ½ hr.

Mushrooms in Olive Oil

½ lb small button mushrooms
3 Tblsp olive oil
1 Tblsp water
salt, pepper
½ tsp dried thyme
2 cloves garlic, crushed
4 Tblsp chopped parsley
juice of 1 lemon

Wash and dry the mushrooms. Pour oil and water into a deep frying pan. Stir in all the remaining ingredients except the mushrooms and bring to the boil. Add the mushrooms and simmer for 10 mins until mushrooms are tender. Turn over occasionally.

Pour into serving dish and allow to cool. Serve cold.

Onions and Potatoes

¾ lb button onions
1 lb new potatoes, scraped and diced, or old potatoes, peeled
1 oz vegan margarine
1 tsp sugar
½ pt vegetable stock
salt
1 Tblsp chopped parsley

Blanch the onions by putting them in a pan of cold water and bringing them to the boil, strain. Place in a flameproof casserole with margarine, sugar, salt and stock. Boil gently until onions are tender and stock has reduced by half. Cook potatoes in boiling salt water. Drain and add to onions. Mix and sprinkle with parsley. Serve.

Parsnips Mashed

1 lb parsnips
2 oz vegan margarine
1 tsp salt, black pepper

Peel and quarter parsnips. Put in a pan with cold water. Cover and boil gently for 40 mins. Drain. Return to gentle heat for a

minute to dry off moisture, do not allow to stick or burn.
Mash parsnips with margarine and seasoning.
Serve very hot.

Peperoni

2 green and 2 red peppers, deseeded and thinly sliced
1 oz vegan margarine
1 onion, sliced
1 clove garlic, crushed
pepper, salt

Prepare and blanch the peppers. Melt the margarine in a small
pan, add onions and garlic and cook slowly until soft. Add the
peppers and seasoning and cook until tender.

Green Pepper with Tomato and Avocado

1 green pepper, deseeded, chopped and blanched
6 large ripe tomatoes
1 avocado, diced
2 spring onions, chopped
2 Tblsp French Dressing (p.77)

Scald and skin tomatoes, cut off tops and remove seeds.
Mix together prepared avocado, pepper, and onion. Moisten
with French Dressing. Fill the tomatoes and replace the lids.
Serve.

Peas with Spring Onions

1 lb young green peas
6 small spring onions, cut in 2-in lengths
¼ cos lettuce, shredded
¼ pt cold water
bouquet garni
1 tsp sugar
½ oz vegan margarine
salt

Put peas in a pan with spring onions, lettuce, herbs, sugar and
½ margarine. Add the water, cover pan with a deep plate filled

with cold water – this causes steam to condense as the peas cook. Cook for 20 mins. Two mins before serving remove bouquet garni, add remaining margarine and salt. Mix well.

Turn into a hot serving dish.

Pickled Cauliflower and Red Cabbage

> 1 cauliflower
> ½ red *or* white cabbage
> 4 Tblsp/3 oz salt
> 1½ pt cold water
> ½ pt white vinegar
> 1 dried chilli pepper pod

Wash cauliflower and separate into florets. Cut cabbage in thick slices in one direction and then in thick slices in the other direction. Leave it in chunks. Pack into a large glass jar, alternate layers of cauliflower and cabbage chunks.

Mix salt, water and vinegar. Pour the liquid over the vegetables and bury chilli pod in the jar. Close the lid tightly and store in a warm place for 10 days.

Potato Balls

Peel potatoes and scoop out potato balls with a cutter. Either plain boil them and toss in melted margarine, or sauté them. Serve sprinkled with chopped parsley.

Potato and Celery

> 3 medium potatoes
> 1 head celery
> 1 oz vegan margarine
> 1 shallot, chopped
> salt, black pepper
> parsley, chopped to garnish

Peel potatoes, trim celery, cut into strips ⅛ inch thick by 2 ins long. Keep potatoes in bowl of water. Heat margarine in flameproof casserole, add celery and shallot, cover and shake over heat for 4 mins. Do not allow vegetables to colour. Drain and dry potatoes. Put them in the casserole and season to taste. Cover with greaseproof paper and lid. Cook on top of stove or in the oven (350°F, 180°C, Mk 4) until potatoes are tender (10 mins)

Garnish with parsley and serve.

Potato Dumplings

> 2 Tblsp left-over mashed potatoes
> 1 Dsp flour

Mix thoroughly and form into golf ball size. Drop into soups and stews and cook for 10 mins.

Potatoes with Mushroom Sauce

> 1½ lb new potatoes
> 1 oz vegan margarine
> 1 onion, chopped finely
> ¼ lb dark mushrooms, chopped
> 1 Tblsp wholemeal flour
> ¾ pt vegetable stock
> 1 small bay leaf
> 1 Dsp mint, chopped

Prepare the sauce: melt margarine and add onion and cook for 2 mins, then add mushrooms and cook for 3 mins. Stir in flour and stock. Stir until sauce boils. Add bay leaf and cook gently for 8 mins.

Scrape the potatoes and boil them. Drain them and add to the sauce.

Add the mint and serve.

Potato and Onion

Slice and fry 1 onion until brown and then remove from pan. Sauté the potatoes. When these are brown add the onion slices and serve.

Sauté Potatoes

> 1½ lb potatoes
> 2 Tblsp oil
> 1 oz vegan margarine
> salt, pepper
> 1 Dsp chopped parsley

Scrub potatoes and boil in their jackets until tender. Drain, peel and slice. Heat oil in a frying pan, when it is hot add margarine. Slip in the potatoes all at once. Add seasoning and sauté until golden brown and crisp, occasionally turning them. Remove and sprinkle with parsley.

Potato Scones

> 1½ lb floury freshly boiled potatoes
> 6 oz plain wholemeal flour
> salt

Crush and sieve potatoes on to a floured board. Add salt. Work in flour gradually, kneading gently. Roll out thinly. Cut into rounds the size of a dinner plate and mark into quarters. Bake on a moderately hot griddle for 10 mins. Turn once.

Rice Baked

> 1 lb long-grain rice
> 2 tsp salt
> ¼ tsp pepper
> 2 pt vegetable stock
> 8 lemon wedges
> paprika

Put the rice, salt and pepper into a lightly greased casserole dish. Pour over boiling vegetable stock. Cover tightly and bake in oven (350°F, 180°C, Mk 4) for 40 mins.

Dip edge of each lemon wedge in paprika and use to decorate baked rice.

Rice with Dates and Almonds

> 1 lb brown rice
> salt
> water
> 4 oz blanched almonds, halved
> 4 oz vegan margarine
> 2 oz raisins
> 4 oz dates, chopped
> ¾ cup water

Boil the rice for 45 mins in salted water until tender. Drain and keep warm.

Fry the almonds in 2 oz margarine until golden. Add raisins and dates. Stir over moderate heat for a few mins. Add 4 fluid oz (¾ of a teacup) of water and simmer gently for 15 mins until the dates are soft and the water has been absorbed.

Melt 1 oz margarine in a heavy saucepan. Add ½ the rice and spread the date and almond mixture over. Cover with remaining rice and dot with last 1 oz margarine. Cover with greaseproof paper and a tight fitting lid and steam over low heat for 30 mins.

Pumpkin Mashed

> 1 lb pumpkin
> 1 oz vegan margarine
> 1 tsp cinnamon
> salt, pepper

Peel pumpkin and remove pips. Cut into chunks and boil for 15 mins until tender. Drain well. Return to gentle heat for a minute to dry off moisture, do not allow to stick or burn.

Mash pumpkin with margarine, cinnamon and seasoning. Serve very hot.

Sprouting Beans

Beans which can be used for sprouting include Mung Beans, Aduki Beans, Alfalfa and Fenugreek seeds. Beans must be in prime condition, not old, broken or split.

Take a 1 pt (¾ litre) glass jar, a piece of muslin and an elastic band. Wash the beans and soak overnight in water. The beans increase in size; 3 rounded Tblsp of Mung Beans will produce 2 cupfuls of sprouts.

Drain the beans and wash in fresh clean water. Put the beans in the clean jar and cover with muslin and secure with the elastic band.

Place the jar in a warm dark place. Rinse the beans twice a day by running cold water through the muslin and draining it out. Excess water must be drained off or the beans will go mouldy.

Within 3–6 days sprouts will be ready to eat.

Sprouts can be used in salads or lightly stir-fried. They can be added to sauces or casseroles or baked in scones.

They keep for several days in the refrigerator. Rinse before use.

Sunflower Seed Patties

  4 oz sunflower seeds
  1 onion
  4 oz millet
  2 Tblsp soya sauce
  1 oz wholemeal flour
  1 Tblsp oil

Peel and finely chop or grate the onion. Cook millet in twice the quantity of water or water to cover. Grind or chop the sunflower seeds. Mix seeds, millet, onion and soya sauce.

Shape into small patties and coat with flour. Fry in oil on both sides until brown.

Tomato and Onion

  1 lb tomatoes, skinned, deseeded and sliced
  1 large onion, sliced into rings
  1 Tblsp oil
  pepper, salt

Fry onion rings until just brown. Add tomatoes and season to taste. Cover pan and cook for 2–3 mins until tomatoes are soft.

Tomato Sambal

        3 tomatoes, skinned and chopped
        1 medium onion, chopped finely
        3 coriander leaves, chopped
        1 Tblsp lemon juice
        pinch of sugar
        salt to taste

Mix all ingredients together and serve with vegetable curry.

Tomatoes Spiced

        14 oz can tomatoes
        1 clove garlic, crushed in ½ tsp salt
        1 tsp sugar
        ¼ pt vegetable stock

Put all ingredients into a pan and simmer until mixture is thick
and pulpy.
    Alternatively instead of garlic use ½ tsp allspice.

Turnips with Onions

        1½ lb small turnip
        1 medium onion
        2 oz vegan margarine
        salt, ground pepper

Peel turnip and cut into ¼-inch slices. Boil in salt water until
tender, then drain. Slice onion in thin rings and brown in melted
margarine. Add onions to turnips and season.
    Toss together and serve hot.

Puddings and Desserts
with Sauces

Aduki Bean Slice

Filling:
2 oz Aduki beans
4 oz apples
1 tsp cinnamon

Base and Topping:
4 oz oats
1 Tblsp vegetable oil
2 oz coconut *or* ground nuts

Soak the Aduki beans then cook for 30 mins. Slice the apples thinly. Mash beans and apples together and add cinnamon. Heat oven to 370°F, 190°C, Mk 5.

Mix all the base ingredients together in a bowl. Oil a sponge tin. Place ½ mixture on the base. Add filling. Cover with topping. Bake for 30 mins until brown.

Serve with liquidised Apricot Compôte (p.98), or an orange or lemon fruit sauce (p.111).

Apple Crumble

Filling:
2–3 large cooking apples
½ tsp cinnamon
2 oz brown sugar

Topping:
6 oz wholemeal flour
3 oz vegan margarine
pinch salt
3 oz brown sugar

Peel, core and slice apples into a casserole dish. Mix together sugar and cinnamon and stir into apples.

Sieve flour and salt into a mixing bowl. Rub in the margarine until mixture resembles fine breadcrumbs. Add sugar and mix well. Sprinkle over apples. Cook in pre-heated oven at 350°F, 180°C, Mk 4 for 20 mins.

Apple Short

> 3 cooking apples, peeled and sliced
> 8 oz brown sugar
> ½ cup water
> 2 oz wholemeal flour
> 4 oz vegan margarine

Place apples in a casserole dish and sprinkle with a little sugar. Add water. Mix together sugar, flour and margarine and cover the apples with this paste, pressing it down firmly. Bake in a slow oven 300°F, 150°C, Mk 2. To be properly cooked the juice should ooze up through the topping, making a toffee-like substance.

Serve with Coconut Cream (p.110).

Apple and Quince Pie

> 1 lb cooking apples
> 1 lb quinces
> ½ lemon
> 6 oz sugar to taste
> 4 oz pastry

Core and slice quinces, chop finely. Put in a saucepan with a few strips lemon rind, cover with water and stew gently until quinces are cooked. Remove lemon rind, add 3 oz sugar to sweeten, and juice of ½ lemon. Peel, core and slice apples and arrange alternate layers of apples and quince in pie-dish, sprinkle each layer of apples with remaining sugar. Half-fill the pie-dish with cold water. Cover the pie with rolled-out pastry and cook in hot oven 450°F, 230°C, Mk 6 for 15 mins, reduce heat and bake for further 20 mins until fruit is cooked.

Serve with custard (p.144).

Apple and Rhubarb Crumble

>   1 lb cooking apples
>   1 lb rhubarb
>   6 oz brown sugar
>   6 oz wholemeal flour
>   3 oz vegan margarine

Clean and trim rhubarb and cut into 1-inch pieces. Peel, core and chop apples. Mix in pie-dish and add 3 oz sugar to taste.

Mix flour, remaining sugar and margarine until they resemble breadcrumbs. Sprinkle over fruit. Bake in oven, 350°F, 180°C, Mk 4, until brown.

Apricot Compôte

>   8 oz dried apricots
>   4 oz sugar
>   1 cinnamon stick
>   1 orange rind and juice
>   1 pt natural orange *or* apple juice

Soak all together overnight. Transfer to pan and cook for 30 mins. Remove cinnamon stick.

Serve hot or cold.

Avocado and Fruit Sweet   *

>   2 avocados
>   2 peaches
>   4 oz grapes
>   4 oz strawberries
>   8 oz sugar
>   ½ pt water
>   2 Tblsp lemon juice
>   4 Tblsp golden syrup

Dissolve sugar in water over gentle heat and boil for 2 mins. Pour over peaches to loosen skin. Remove skin. Halve peaches and remove stones, slice into sugar syrup and chill. Peel and stone avocados and slice. Halve and deseed grapes. Mix together all the fruit and put into glasses. Spoon over syrup. Mix lemon juice and golden syrup and warm until blended. Spoon over fruit.

Baked Bananas

4 bananas
2 oz margarine
2 oz brown sugar
1 lemon

Skin bananas and put in dish, sprinkle over sugar and add margarine and lemon rind. Cook in moderate oven (350°F, 180°C, Mk 4) for 10 mins until soft.

Serve with a little lemon juice.

Baked Banana Pie

8 oz short crust pastry
8 bananas
6 oz orange juice
2 tsp lime juice
4 oz sugar
1 tsp nutmeg
1 Tblsp arrowroot
2 oz margarine
4 oz chilled coconut cream

Line pie-dish with pastry, prick, and bake blind in hot oven (450°F, 230°C, Mk 6) for 15 mins. Allow to cool. Peel bananas and put in well-oiled baking tin. Mix orange juice, lime juice, sugar and nutmeg. Pour over bananas. Bake in moderate oven, 350°F, 180°C, Mk 4, for 15 mins until bananas are golden. Remove bananas carefully and allow to cool. Thicken syrup with arrowroot mixed in a little water. Add margarine and beat well. Arrange bananas on baked pie shell. Pour thickened sauce over bananas.

Serve with Coconut Cream. (p.110).

Grilled Bananas

The bananas must be firm and not overripe. Slit them through the skin down one side, but do not peel them. Grill in the skins until they are charred and soft, turning them a few times. Remove skins carefully so as not to break them.

Serve with sugar and wedges of lime or lemon.

Baked Fruit

            4 pears, peeled but not cored
            4 apples, peeled halfway and cored
            3 oz raisins
            3 oz brown sugar
            1 oz vegan margarine
            ¼ pt orange juice
            ¼ pt water
            ½ oz cornflour

Stuff the centre of the apples with raisins, sprinkle on 1 oz of the sugar and top with a nut of margarine. Put the fruit into the pan. Add the orange juice, water and rest of the sugar, cover and cook gently until tender, basting occasionally. When cooked remove from the pan and put into the serving dish. Mix the cornflour smoothly with a little water. Add to the syrup and boil until it thickens. Pour over the fruit.

Balouza

            4 oz cornflour
            2 pt water
            8 oz sugar
            ¼ pt orange blossom *or* rose water
            2 oz almonds, blanched and chopped

Mix cornflour to a smooth paste with a little water in a large pan. Add the rest of the water and the sugar and stir vigorously until dissolved. Bring to the boil slowly, stirring continuously until mixture thickens – it should cling and coat the spoon.

Stir in orange blossom or rose water and cook for 2–3 mins.

Add the chopped nuts, stir well and pour into a glass bowl. Chill.

Exotic Fruit Salad
Serves 8 ✱

> 2 apples
> 2 pears
> 1 pomegranate *or* 4 passion fruit
> 1 litre pure mixed fruit juice
> 2 tangerines
> 2 kiwi fruit
> 8 seedless grapes
> 2 Tblsp lemon juice
> 4 fresh figs *or* 1 pawpaw (papaya)

Core and slice the apples unpeeled. Peel core and slice the pears. Sprinkle both with lemon juice. Peel tangerines, segment and remove pips. Peel and slice kiwi fruit. Halve grapes if large. Break pomegranate into small pieces or scoop out passion fruit. Slice figs or peel, deseed and dice pawpaw.

Combine fruit and cover with fruit juice.

Serve with Coconut Cream (p.110).

Fresh Fruit Compôte

> 1 cooking apple
> 1 peach
> 2 apricots
> 1 pear
> 2 plums
> cupful of strawberries

Syrup

Boil water with half its volume of sugar and add lemon juice to taste: 2 cups of water to 1 cup of sugar.

Wash, peel, core or stone and slice all the fruit. Put the fruit in a large pan with the syrup. Bring to the boil and simmer for 15 mins until fruit is soft.

Serve cold with Coconut Cream. (p.110)

Frumenty

> 7 oz wholemeal grain
> 1½ pt water
> salt
> 1 oz brown sugar
> ½ tsp ground cinnamon
> ground ginger
> 3 oz currants
> 1 oz walnuts, chopped to garnish

Simmer wholemeal grain in water with salt for 1½ hrs until tender and the water has been absorbed. Mix together sugar, spices and currants and cook for further 5 mins. Turn into heated serving dish, sprinkle with nuts.

Serve hot or cold with stewed fruit.

Glacé Fruits

> 1 seedless satsuma
> 12 black grapes
> 3 oz sugar
> 3 Tblsp water

Peel satsuma and divide into segments, removing as much pith as possible.

Cut grapes almost in half lengthwise, removing the pips.

Place sugar and water in a small saucepan and bring slowly to the boil, make sure the sugar has all dissolved before it boils. Once the sugar has dissolved, do not stir, boil until syrup begins to turn a pale straw colour. Immediately drop pieces of fruit one at a time into the syrup, remove and place on a board. Spoon any remaining syrup over the fruit before it sets.

Arrange fruit with a satsuma segment inside a grape and place in a paper sweet-case to dry and set.

Serve at the end of a meal with coffee.

Granitas

Granitas are Italian Water Ices and can be served as a slushy drink or as a dessert. Known in Spanish as Sorbetes – see also Sorbets.

Melon Granita

1 ripe Honeydew melon
2 oz icing sugar
juice of 2 lemons
fresh mint to garnish

Quarter melon, remove pips. Scoop the flesh into a blender. Add the icing sugar and lemon juice then blend to a smooth cream. Pour into a container and freeze.

Leave mixture at room temperature for 15 mins, then crush it by hand or in the blender.

Serve decorated with mint.

Variations

Add a pinch of ground ginger when serving.

Decorate with chopped nuts.

Other fruit may be used: strawberries, apples etc.

Earl Grey Granita

1 pt water
3 oz syrup
3 lemons, grated rind and juice
3 Tblsp Earl Grey tea leaves
lemon wedges, to decorate

Put water, syrup and lemon rind in a pan and bring to the boil. Boil rapidly for 5 mins, then add the tea. Cover and leave to infuse for 20–30 mins, depending on strength preferred.

Strain into a container, then add lemon juice. Stir well. Cover and freeze. To serve, thaw for 20 mins, then crush by hand or in a blender.

Serve decorated with lemon wedges.

Variations

Try other scented or fruit-flavoured teas.

Grated Apples

6 eating apples
juice of 1 lemon
3 Tblsp icing sugar
juice of 1 orange
2 ice cubes, crushed
1 lemon, cut into wedges to garnish

Peel and grate the apples into a bowl, add the lemon juice to prevent them discolouring. Add sugar to taste and orange juice. Mix, and chill for a few hours.

Before serving add the crushed ice and decorate with lemon.

Hawaiian Shortcake

8 oz sugar
¾ cup finely chopped pineapple
2 tsp cornflour
2 ripe bananas, mashed
2 Tblsp lemon juice
2 passion fruit (optional)

Put the sugar, pineapple and cornflour in a pan. Stir over the heat until it thickens. Cool. When cool add the mashed bananas, passion fruit and lemon juice, and place in serving dish.

Mixed Fruit Salad

4 oz dried apricots
4 oz dried prunes
4 oz dried figs
1 pt natural orange *or* apple juice
4 oz walnut halves

Soak dried fruit in juice overnight. Transfer to pan and warm gently for 10 mins.

Serve warm sprinkled with walnuts.

Serve for breakfast or as a sweet.

Pear Charlotte

    1 lb pears
    4 Tblsp apricot jam
    2 oz melted vegan margarine
    5 Tblsp brown sugar
    6 slices bread

Peel, core and slice pears. Put half in a well-greased oven-proof dish. Sprinkle with 2 Tblsp sugar and spread with 2 Tblsp jam. Cover with remaining pears, 2 Tblsp sugar and jam. Remove crusts from bread and cut each slice into 4 triangles. Dip into melted margarine and arrange on top of the dish, covering the contents completely. Sprinkle with remaining sugar. Bake at 375°F, 190°C, Mk 5, for 30–40 mins until crisp and golden.

Serve hot with Coconut Cream (p.110) or Soya Custard (p.144).

Raisin Lattice Pie   *

    Case
    8 oz wholemeal flour
    ½ tsp salt
    4 oz whipped white cooking fat
    2 Tblsp water

    Filling
    2 oranges
    1 oz cornflour
    8 oz seedless raisins
    2 oz brown sugar
    2 oz vegan margarine

Sieve flour and salt into a bowl, add fat and water and mix until a ball of dough is formed. Knead lightly. Line a 9-inch sandwich tin with three quarters of the pastry. Roll the rest out and cut into 6 inch by ½ inch strips. Dampen pastry edges.

Grate zest and squeeze oranges. Make the juice from the oranges up to ½ pt with water. Blend the cornflour with 2 Tblsp of liquid. Boil the remainder with the raisins and the sugar. Add the moistened cornflour and bring to the boil, stirring continuously. Add margarine and orange zest, cool and pour into pastry case. Place strips of pastry, twisted in a lattice pattern over filling. Brush with a little juice.

Bake in oven 400°F, 200°C, Mk 6 for 30 mins.

Serve with Coconut Cream (p.110).

Prunes Stuffed with Walnuts

> 1 lb prunes
> walnut halves, same number as prunes
> boiling tea
> ½ pt water
> 2 Tblsp sugar
> 1 Tblsp lemon juice

Wash the prunes. Pour strained hot tea over them and soak overnight. Boil the prunes in the tea until tender. Cool and remove stones. Stuff them with half a walnut.

Bring the water, sugar and lemon juice to the boil. Drop in the stuffed prunes and simmer gently, covered, for ½ hr. The walnuts become impregnated with the syrup.

Allow to cool and serve with Coconut Cream (p.110) or Soya Custard (p.144).

Rice Pudding

> ¼ lb ground rice
> 2¼ pt water
> 4 oz sugar
> 1 tsp caraway seeds
> 1 tsp fennel seeds
> 1 tsp aniseed
> pinch of ground ginger
> almonds, blanched and chopped *or* hazelnuts to garnish

Mix the ground rice to a smooth paste with some cold water. Add the sugar, caraway seeds, fennel seeds and aniseed and mix well. Bring the remaining water to the boil with the ginger. Add the ground rice paste gradually, stirring with a wooden spoon. Bring to the boil and allow to simmer until it thickens, about 1 hr. Pour into serving bowl.

Allow to cool and chill.

Serve decorated with nuts.

Rhubarb and Mandarin Tart

Pastry
12 oz wholemeal flour
½ tsp salt
3 oz white vegetable fat
3 Tblsp cold water

Filling
½ lb rhubarb, peeled
1 tin unsweetened mandarins
2 oz sugar
1 tsp cornflour

Mix flour, salt and fat till it is like crumbs. Add water until firm dough is formed. Knead lightly on a floured board. Divide in two. Roll out into 2 circles, one larger. Use larger one to line 8-inch pie-dish and smaller one for lid.

Drain the mandarins and keep the juice. Cut rhubarb into 1-inch lengths. Place both in a pastry case. Sprinkle with sugar. Sieve cornflour on top.

Dampen pastry edges, cover with lid and seal well. Cut steam vent in top. Decorate with pastry trimmings. Brush with mandarin juice. Bake in hot oven (425°F, 220°C, Mk 7 for 15 mins), then reduce heat for 20 mins until golden.

Sesame Apples

1 Tblsp sesame seeds
4 eating apples
1 Tblsp cornflour
4 oz sugar
2 Tblsp oil

Spread sesame seeds on a sheet of foil and toast under grill until golden. Peel, core and cut apples into small chunks. Toss in cornflour. Dissolve the sugar slowly in warm oil until it becomes a thick syrup, with a little oil floating on top and pale golden brown. Drop in a few apple chunks at a time. Remove with a fork and place in a wire basket. Dip in and out of a bowl of iced water to set like toffee. Place on individual plates. Sprinkle with sesame seeds.

Sorbet

Sorbet is derived from the Spanish name given to Water Ices and is similar to the Italian Granitas. See under Granitas.

Orange Sorbet

> 1 pt orange juice *or* ¾ pt orange juice and ¼ pt lemon juice
> to give tang
> ¾ lb sugar
> 1½ pt water
> 1 Tblsp orange blossom water

Boil the water and sugar together for 5 mins until sugar is dissolved. Remove from heat, allow to cool and stir in the orange juice and orange blossom water.

Pour into container and freeze. Beat lightly with a fork every ½ hour to reduce the size of the crystals. Transfer to the refrigerator compartment 20 mins before serving.

Serve in scooped-out orange or lemon halves.

Lemon Sorbet

> ½ pt lemon juice
> 1½ pt water
> ½ lb sugar
> 1 Tblsp orange blossom water

Make in the same way as Orange Sorbet.

Strawberry Sorbet

> ¾ lb strawberry purée (with added sugar, optional)
> 2 Tblsp lemon juice
> 4 Tblsp orange juice

Blend fruit juices and purée and pour into container. Cover and freeze. When ice crystals form remove and beat thoroughly. Return to container and freeze until firm.

Strawberry and Pineapple Dessert

8 oz strawberries
1 small pineapple
angelica
3 oranges
1 lemon

Wash strawberries and halve them. Peel pineapple, cut into slices and remove core. Dice. Squeeze the juice from the oranges and lemon and chill. Place the strawberries and pineapple in individual dishes, pour over the juice and decorate with chopped angelica.

Stuffed Peaches

4 peaches raw *or* canned
4 oz desiccated coconut
4 oz vegan margarine
4 oz brown sugar

Halve and remove stones from peaches. Cream together coconut, margarine and sugar and fill centre of peaches. Bake for 30 mins (375°F, 190°C, Mk 4).

Soya Pudding

1 pt soya milk
1½ oz pudding rice
3 cloves
¼ tsp nutmeg

Place dry ingredients in a greased ovenproof dish.
Pour on the soya milk. Cover and bake at 300°F, 150°C, Mk 2 for 2–2½ hrs. Remove cover for the last ½ hr.
Serve hot or cold with stewed fruit.

Tofu 'Cheesecake'

Base
8 oz flour
4 oz sugar
½ tsp salt
¼ tsp cinnamon
2 Tblsp oil
2 oz vegan margarine
2 Tblsp water

Topping
1 pkt tofu
2 Tblsp lemon juice
2 Tblsp oil
8 oz sugar
½ tsp salt
1½ tsp vanilla
2 oz soya milk

Use a 9-inch flan dish. Mix flour, sugar, salt and cinnamon. Work in oil and margarine to a crumble. Add water. Press into bottom and sides of oiled flan dish. Bake for 10 mins.

Combine topping ingredients in a blender, add the milk only if needed. The mixture should be thick and creamy. Pour into the partially cooked base.

Bake for ½ hr at 350°F, 180°C, Mk 4.

Serve decorated with fruit or nuts.

Sauces

Sauces add moisture and flavour to give the finishing touch to a dessert.

Coconut Cream Sauce

7 oz pkt coconut cream
½ pt very hot water

Break the coconut cream into small lumps, if very hard, grate. Cover with hot water and stir until the lumps dissolve. Add the remaining hot water and beat until it forms a thick creamy sauce.

Serve hot or cold.

If the coconut cream is chilled it may set. Before serving stir in 1 Dsp of very hot water to reconstitute.

Fruit Sauce

> 2 tsp cornflour
> ½ pt fruit juice from canned fruit e.g. pineapple, mandarins
> zest and juice of ½ lemon *or* 1 orange
> 1 oz vegan margarine

Mix cornflour with 2 Tblsp juice. Bring remaining juice to the boil and stir in cornflour paste. Stir in zest and juice. Cook, stirring continuously until thick and smooth, 2–3 mins. Beat in margarine.

Serve with fruit tarts or pies.

Bread and Pastry

Bread
Makes 3 1-lb loaves

Part of the success in bread-making depends on keeping everything warm. The dough should be relatively soft but not sticky and should not be overstretched by allowing it to rise too high above the edge of the tin. Bread should be cooked rapidly in a hot oven.

> 3 lb flour (mix 1½ lb brown wholemeal and 1½ lb plain white)
> 3 oz fresh yeast *or* 3 tsp fresh, granulated yeast
> 1½ pt warm water
> 3 tsp sugar
> 3 tsp salt
> 3 oz vegetable oil
> sesame seeds

Dissolve yeast in 1 pt of water, add sugar and allow to ferment in a warm place.

Place flour and salt in the mixing bowl and warm in the oven, 250°F, 130°C, Mk ½, for 10 mins. Rub in the oil until granular. Mix in the yeast ferment and add water until the flour reaches a soft dough consistency which does not stick to the hands.

Knead well on a floured board or table top for 5–10 mins.

Replace in the mixing bowl and cover, place in a warm spot for about 30 mins until the dough has doubled in size. If an even texture is required, the kneading can be repeated and the dough allowed to rise again.

Dust 3 1-lb bread tins with flour, or if the dough was a little sticky, grease with oil. Divide the dough into 3 equal portions and place in tins. Allow to rise to double their size in a warm place.

Heat the oven to 475°F, 240°C, Mk 9. Brush the top of the bread with a little warm water and sprinkle with sesame seeds.

Cook the bread in the middle of the oven for 25 mins. Then reduce the heat to 425°F, 210°C, Mk 7 for 10–15 mins.

When the bread is cooked the crusts should contract from the edges of the tin without sticking. Turn out on to cooling trays.

(It freezes well.)

Pitta Bread
Makes 12

> 1½ lb wholemeal flour
> ½ oz salt
> 1 sachet activated dry yeast
> 1 Tblsp oil
> ¾ pt water

In a large bowl mix together flour, salt and yeast.

Mix in oil and then the water. Beat until a smooth dough is formed. Cover with a plastic bag and leave in a warm place to rise.

When it has risen to twice its size, knead well on a lightly floured board. Do not add more flour.

Break the dough into 6-cm (4-inch) balls and dust with flour and leave to rise for 20 mins. Roll out the balls to oval shapes.

Place the shapes on an oiled baking tray and bake for 9 mins in a hot oven (425°F, 220°C, Mk 7).

Chapattis
Makes 4

> 2 oz chapatti flour
> ½ tsp oil
> salt
> ½ tsp water

Mix the ingredients together and add water to make a soft dough. Knead well. Add a little more oil at the end. Roll out very thin. Cook in a frying pan without any added oil over a low heat. Layer up and cover to keep warm.

Parathe
Makes 4

> 2 oz chapatti flour
> salt
> ½ tsp oil
> ½ tsp water
> ½ oz vegan margarine

Mix the flour, salt and nearly all the oil together and add a little water to make a soft dough. Knead well and add a little more oil at the end.

Roll out into an oval. Pinch waist to form a figure 8 shape. Spread with margarine. Sprinkle over with flour. Fold over. Repeat once more.

Cook in a dry pan. Turn after 1 min. Spread on a little oil if it sticks.

Puri
Makes 4

> 2 oz chapatti flour
> 1 litre oil
> ½ tsp chilli powder
> ½ tsp turmeric
> salt, pepper
> ½ tsp water

Mix chapatti flour with a very little oil, ¼ tsp, add chilli powder, turmeric and salt and pepper. Add enough water to make a stiff dough. Knead well, at the end add a little more oil.

Take walnut-size pieces and roll to 3-inch rounds.

Fry in hot deep oil, pressing them down below the surface at the beginning.

Pastry

Vegan pastry can be bought deep-frozen. If possible make your own; this is a simple method.

> 8 oz flour
> 5 oz vegan margarine
> 2 Tblsp water

Put the margarine with 2 Tblsp flour and the water in a deep mixing bowl. Cream the ingredients with a fork until well mixed. Work in the remaining flour to a firm dough. Turn on to a floured surface and knead lightly until smooth. Chill for 30 mins before using. Roll out to required shape.

Bake in pre-heated oven, 400°F, 200°C, Mk 6, until golden.

Pastry with Oil

8 oz flour
5 Tblsp vegetable oil
5 Tblsp cold water
¼ tsp salt

Whisk the oil and water together in a large bowl, until evenly blended. Gradually stir in the flour and salt to form a dough. Turn on to a floured surface. Knead the pastry lightly until smooth and shiny. Roll out and cut to required shape.

Bake in pre-heated oven, 400°F, 200°C, Mk 6 for 20 mins or until golden. This pastry must be mixed quickly and used straight away.

Cakes

Anaesthetic Cake

Makes 1 lb cake

This recipe came from a Greek friend and is so-called because of the strange, but not unpleasant, effect it has of slightly numbing the mouth.

12 oz flour
7 oz sugar
juice of 2 oranges
1 tsp soda bicarbonate
1 Tblsp ground cloves
1 Tblsp ground cinnamon
4 oz vegetable oil
4 oz water
2 oz brandy (optional)
4 oz currants
1 oz walnut pieces

Add the soda bicarbonate to the orange juice.

Add all the ingredients except the flour and mix well. Fold in the flour.

Pour mixture into a 1 lb bread tin. Cook at 400°F, 200°C, Mk 6 for 1 hr.

Bran Fruit Loaf

Makes 2 1-lb loaves

4 oz Allbran
4 oz brown sugar
4 oz sultanas
4 oz currants
2 oz seedless raisins
½ pt soya milk
14 oz wheatmeal self-raising flour

Heat oven to 350°F, 180°C, Mk 4. Grease 2 1-lb bread tins. Soak the Allbran, sugar and dried fruits in the soya milk for

30 mins, or until soya milk has been absorbed. Stir in flour and turn into the bread tins. Bake for 1 hr.

Variations

Dried fruit mixture can be varied. Chopped dates, figs, etc. keeping the quantities.

Up to 2 oz of chopped nuts can be added.

½ tsp allspice and ½ tsp cinnamon can be added.

Date Flapjacks
Makes 15 squares

> 4 oz dates
> 2 oz syrup
> ½ oz malt
> 4 oz rolled oats
> 1 oz vegetable oil

Cover dates with water and boil them in a pan until they become a paste.

Heat oven to 375°F, 190°C, Mk 5.

Heat syrup, malt and oil. Take off heat and add the oats. Oil a swiss-roll tin. Place half the mixture in the bottom and press flat. Spread the date paste over the mixture. Place the other half of the mixture on the top and press flat. Bake for 35 mins until golden.

DO NOT cut or take out of the tin until cool.

Date and Walnut Bread
Makes 1 lb

> 1 lb wholewheat flour
> 1 sachet dried activated yeast
> pinch of salt
> 2 oz dates
> 2 oz walnuts
> ½ pt apple juice

Mix flour, yeast and salt together. Chop up the dates and walnuts and mix into the flour. Mix in the apple juice to form a stiff dough.

Place in a 1 lb bread tin and leave in a warm place to rise.

Heat oven to 400°F, 200°C, Mk 6. When the dough has reached the top of the tin place in the oven. Bake for 35 mins.

Turn out on to cooling rack. Test when cooked by tapping the bottom of the loaf; it should sound hollow when cooked.

Chocolate Squares

Makes 15 squares

> 4 oz rolled oats
> 3 oz coconut
> 6 oz vegan margarine
> 4 oz sugar
> 4 oz flour
> 1 Dsp cocoa
> ½ tsp baking powder

Cream sugar and margarine. Add all the dry ingedients. Mix well. Press the mixture into a greased swiss-roll tin.

Bake in pre-heated oven (375°F, 190°C, Mk 5) for 20 mins. Ice with water icing while hot.

Water Icing:

> 12 oz icing sugar
> ½ tsp vanilla
> 2 Dsp cocoa
> 4 Tblsp hot water

Beat ingredients together until mixture thickens. Pour over hot base.

Allow to cool. Cut into 2-inch squares and lift out of the swiss-roll tin.

Raisin Cookies

Makes about 100 biscuits

> 8 oz vegan margarine
> 8 oz sugar
> 1 Tblsp syrup
> 1 tsp soda bicarbonate
> 1 Tblsp orange juice
> 1 lb flour
> 8 oz dried fruit

Melt the margarine, sugar and syrup together. Mix the soda

bicarbonate into the orange juice and add to the mixture. Cool.

Add flour and fruit and mix well. Form into small balls. Place, well spaced, on a baking tray. Flatten the balls with a fork. Bake in a pre-heated oven, 350°F, 180°C, Mk 4, until golden.

Fruit Loaf

Makes 1 lb

8 oz brown sugar
5 oz water
3 oz raisins
3 oz sultanas
½ tsp nutmeg
3 oz vegan margarine
1 tsp cinnamon
1 tsp ginger
¼ tsp salt
8 oz flour
½ tsp baking powder
1 tsp soda bicarbonate

Boil together sugar, water, fruit, nutmeg, margarine, cinnamon, ginger, and salt for 3 mins. Allow to cool. Sift together flour, baking powder and soda bicarbonate. Fold the flour into the fruit mixture.

Pre-heat oven to 300°F, 150°C, Mk 2. Bake in a greased 1 lb bread tin for 1 hr.

Shortbread

2 oz cornflour
4 oz flour
4 oz vegan margarine
2 oz caster sugar

Sieve cornflour and flour together. Mix with other ingredients slowly, adding the flour by Tblsp until the mixture is crumbly.

Press into a lightly greased 7-inch round tin. Prick with a fork and score with a knife. Put in the refrigerator for 15 mins.

Bake in pre-heated oven (350°F, 180°C, Mk 4) for 35–40 mins.

Leave until cool. Turn on to kitchen paper.

Ginger Shortbread

          8 oz vegan margarine
          4 oz caster sugar
          2 tsp ground ginger
          10 oz flour
          2 tsp baking powder

Cream margarine and sugar together. Add all dry ingredients.
Press into lightly greased 7-inch round tin.
Bake in oven pre-heated to 350°F, 180°C, Mk 4 for 40 mins.

Topping

          2 tsp ground ginger
          8 oz icing sugar
          4 oz vegan margarine
          6 tsp syrup

Melt all ingredients together and pour over warm shortbread.
Cut while still warm.

Sweetcorn Scones   *Makes 16*

          1 x 7 oz tin sweetcorn
          2 oz vegan margarine
          8 oz flour
          4 tsp baking powder
          ½ tsp salt
          juice from sweetcorn (made up to 4 oz with water)

Drain the tin of sweetcorn and keep the juice.
Rub the margarine into the dry ingredients. Mix in the
sweetcorn. Add the juice and blend into a soft dough.
Turn on to a floured board and shape with floured hands.
Roll out to ¾-1 inch thick. Cut into shapes.
Place on a greased baking sheet. Bake in pre-heated oven,
475°F, 240°C, Mk 9, for 10–12 mins.
Quickness is *essential* in making scones.

Dips

Dips are fun. They provide a snack before a meal, or a nibble at a party, and add variety to a buffet, or a barbecue.

They are served with firm edible Dippits or crudités to dip into the mixture. The first part of this chapter gives recipes for Dippits, the second part recipes for the dips.

Dippits

Melba Toast

Toast thin slices of wholemeal bread in a toaster until brown. Split through the centre of the toast with a bread knife and cut into 4 triangles. Toast raw side of bread under the grill.

Pepperpot Shortbread

> 4 oz flour
> ½ tsp salt
> 1 tsp dry mustard
> 2 oz fine semolina
> ¼ tsp cayenne pepper
> ¼ tsp white pepper
> 4 oz vegan margarine
> 2 Tblsp cold water

Sift dry ingredients together. Rub in margarine until the mixture is like fine breadcrumbs. Mix to a dry dough with water. Turn on to a lightly floured board and knead quickly until smooth. Roll out into a round shape about 8 inches across.

Lift on to a lightly greased baking tray, pinch up the edges and cut into 8 equal triangles. Bake in moderate oven (400°F, 200°C, Mk 5) for 30 mins.

Crudités or Raw Vegetables

Raw vegetables cut into strips can be used with dips, spreads and pâtés.

Suitable vegetables

> carrots
> celery
> fennel
> peppers
> cucumber
> mushrooms
> radishes
> young green beans
> cauliflower florets
> young peas in the pod
> spring onions

Dips

Avocado Dip

> 2 large ripe avocados
> ½ small onion, chopped
> 4 tomatoes, peeled, deseeded and chopped
> 1 green chilli, deseeded and chopped
> juice of 1 lemon
> salt, pepper to taste
> parsley to garnish

Mix together onion, tomatoes, chilli and half the lemon juice and seasoning. Cover and leave to marinate for ½ hour.

Peel avocados and mash. Stir in tomato mixture and the rest

of the lemon juice. An avocado stone in the base of the bowl prevents the mixture going brown.

Garnish with parsley.

Aubergine Dip

> 2 large aubergines
> 1 Tblsp lemon juice
> 1 clove garlic
> 2 Tblsp olive oil
> 2 Tblsp parsley
> salt, pepper to taste

Prick aubergines all over. Roll up in tin foil and bake in oven, 375°F, 190°C, Mk 5, for 45 mins. Cool, peel and chop, then place in blender with other ingredients until smooth and creamy. Season to taste.

Place in earthenware dish, cover and chill.

Garnish with parsley.

Aubergine with Tahini

> 3 large aubergines
> 3 cloves of garlic, crushed
> ¼ pt tahini paste
> juice of 3 lemons
> ½ tsp ground cumin
> salt to taste
> 2 Tblsp chopped parsley, black olives, tomato slices to garnish

Sear aubergines over a fire or under a grill until the skins become black and blistered and the flesh is soft. Rub the skins off under cold water. Gently squeeze out as much juice as is possible, this juice is bitter.

Mash the aubergines and add the garlic and other ingredients and mash to a creamy purée. Alternatively purée in a blender.

Pour into a serving bowl and decorate with parsley, black olives and tomato slices.

Butter Bean and Black Olive Dip

      4 oz butter beans, cooked and drained
      12 black olives, stoned and mashed
      2 Tblsp olive oil
      2 Tblsp lemon juice
      salt, pepper to taste
      Tabasco sauce
      crisp lettuce leaves
      chopped chives

Mash together beans and olives, and add oil, lemon juice, salt and pepper and a drop or two of Tabasco sauce.

Serve on crisp lettuce with chopped leaves sprinkled over.

(This freezes well.)

Nut Butter Dip

      5 oz of any of the following nuts, either raw or roasted:
      peanuts
      cashew
      hazelnuts
      walnuts
      Brazil
      pecan
      pistachio
      almonds
      or a mixture of these.
      Vegetable oil if needed
      salt to taste

Grind nuts in a blender or food processor to a smooth paste or a crunchy texture. Help the mixture on to the blades, first switching the machine off. Use oil if needed.

Season to taste.

(This mixture keeps well when stored in a sealed jar.)

The Vegan Barbecue

On warm summer evenings it is relaxing to build a fire and cook in the open. Children especially love the novelty of cooking outside and join in enthusiastically. The smell of smoke and cooking is tantalising and there is something special about eating outside. Part of the enjoyment of eating food cooked over an open fire is the smoky flavour imparted to it. A handful of chopped rosemary sprinkled over the coals scents the smoke with a lovely smell.

Many vegetables can be cooked in the hot coals of the fire for example:

Jacket Potatoes

Use small to medium size and wrap in tinfoil.

Onions

Leave in their skins and wrap in tinfoil. Remove the outer skins when serving.

Mushrooms

Use button mushrooms or slice large ones, add 1 oz vegan margarine to 4 oz mushrooms and parcel in tinfoil.

Corn-on-the-Cob

Leave in the husk and wrap in tinfoil. Before serving remove the husk and spread with vegan margarine.

Chestnuts

In season, pricked and roasted chestnuts are delicious and give off a lovely smell.

Marinades

Food soaked in a marinade before cooking is improved in flavour and texture. Also use the marinade to pour over food that is cooking to prevent it from burning, or use as a sauce or dip.

> 4 Tblsp vegetable oil
> juice of 1 lemon
> 1 Tblsp soya sauce
> 1 Tblsp vinegar
> 1 Tblsp tomato sauce
> 1 tsp dry mustard
> 1 tsp mixed herbs
> 1 Tblsp home-made chutney *or* ½ tsp Marmite *or* yeast
>   extract
> salt, pepper

Mix all the ingredients together and shake well.
    Soak the food in the marinade for at least ½ hr.

Nut Cutlets

> 4 oz peanuts, ground
> 3 oz wholemeal breadcrumbs
> ½ tsp thyme
> 3 Tblsp soya flour
> salt, pepper
> juice of ½ lemon
> 2 tsp soya sauce
> water to bind

Mix all the dry ingredients together. Add juice, soya sauce and enough water to bind. Form into sausages or burger shapes. Brush with oil and barbecue.

Lentil Sausages

8 oz lentils
2 tomatoes
1 tsp mixed herbs
2 tsp soya flour
½ pt water
1 Dsp yeast extract
2 tsp porridge oats
salt, pepper to taste

Soak the lentils in the water until soft. Skin and mash the tomatoes. Add remaining ingredients and enough water to make a firm mixture. Shape into sausages, brush with oil and barbecue.

Sweetcorn 'Braai'

4 sweetcorn cobs in their husks
salt, pepper
2 oz vegan margarine

Pull back husks and remove the hairs. Spread the cob with margarine and salt and pepper. Refold husk leaves carefully around the cobs, skewer and roast over the fire, turning frequently until husks are charred.

Remove husks and serve.

Kidney Bean Burgers

8 oz red kidney beans
2 large onions
2 oz fresh parsley
2 oz wholemeal flour
1 Tblsp soya sauce
salt, pepper to taste

Soak the kidney beans overnight and drain. Boil vigorously in plenty of water for 10 mins, then simmer until soft and drain.

Grate the onions and chop the parsley. Mash the beans. Stir in all the ingredients and leave to cool. This mixture will keep in the refrigerator for 1 week. Form into burger-shapes and brush with oil and barbecue.

Kebabs

> 1 lb tofu pressed until firm and cut into 1 inch cubes
> 4 large tomatoes cut into wedges
> ½ lb very small onions *or* onion quarters
> 1 pineapple cut into cubes *or* 1 tin of pineapple pieces
> 1 pepper cut into 1 in squares

Stick two of each ingredient alternately on to 4 skewers and grill over the fire.

Fruit 'Braai'

> 2 eating apples
> 2 pears
> 1 melon
> 4 oz syrup
> 3 Tblsp lemon juice
> 2 oz vegan margarine

Mix syrup, lemon juice and margarine in a saucepan and stir over fire until blended.

Cut apples and pears into wedges, and melon into cubes. Thread on to skewers and dip in the sauce. Grill gently until the fruit is glazed, brushing with sauce and turning frequently to prevent burning.

Bananas

Wrap 4 unskinned bananas in tinfoil and place in the hot coals for 5 mins or until soft.

Small, unripe mangoes can be cooked in the same way.

Other Ideas

Sandwiches and bread can also be toasted over hot coals.

Serve the barbecued food with a variety of salads.

Health food shops sell a variety of meat-like products and sosmix suitable for making into kebabs, hamburgers or sausages. Read the label carefully as some companies use egg for binding.

Coffee can be percolated or water boiled for drinks.

Eating to Survive

This chapter is for those surviving on a tight budget and those who find cooking an unenjoyable chore. The recipes are simple, cheap, quick to make, and of good nutritional value. Recipes in this section serve 1 person, unless otherwise stated.

Breakfast

Fruit

> grapefruit
> ugli fruit
> orange segments
> pawpaw (papaya)
> water-melon
> guavas

Any fruit that is halved, cover with cling film and keep in the fridge. Many fruits are tinned; empty any that is left over from the tin and keep in a covered container in the fridge

Toast

Use sliced wholemeal bread or bread buns, halved. Toast until golden. Spread with vegan margarine and any vegan jams, preserves, marmalades or Marmite. Also butter spreads made of peanuts, hazelnuts or carob.
　On the toast:
　Heated – baked beans, sweetcorn, left-overs, or grilled tofu.

Muesli

This can be bought loose, and in a variety of mixes from the wholefood shops, or in packets from the supermarkets. *Beware*:

milk powder may have been added; ask, or read the ingredients on the side of the packet. Muesli may be eaten on its own but it is rather dry and most people prefer it moistened with soya milk or fruit juice.

Home-made Muesli

1 ½ lb oats
6 oz mixed dry fruit
3 oz Weetaflakes
2–4 oz raw sugar
3 oz bran
2 oz mixed chopped nuts

Mix all the ingredients together. Add the sugar according to taste. Keep in an air-tight container.

Cooked Breakfast

It takes 3–5 minutes to fry any or all of the following in 2 oz of vegetable oil:

wholemeal bread
green peppers
bananas halved lengthways and fried until soft
mushrooms
left-overs
onion rings
sliced tomatoes

Rice Cakes

cooked rice
soya milk
flour
vegetable oil
Marmite *or* tomato sauce

Moisten the cooked rice with a little soya milk and form into small cakes. Roll in the flour. Fry in the hot oil until golden. Eat with Marmite or tomato sauce.

Drinks

A few suggestions:

> cold *or* boiled water
> soya milk flavoured
> plain tea, with a sprig of mint *or* a slice of lemon, hot *or* iced
> black coffee
> pure fruit juices chilled *or* warmed

Snacks or a Light Meal

Soups

Vegetable soups are easy to make but not quick. If soups are bought in tins or packets, read the ingredients as the soup may have been thickened with milk or using animal fat.

Clear Vegetable Soup   *Serves 4*

> 1½ pt vegetable stock *or* stock cube
> ½ oz vegan margarine
> 1 tsp yeast extract
> 1 small bay leaf
> salt, pepper to taste

Boil all the ingredients together for 15 mins. Serve garnished with parsley and with warm wholemeal buns. Any left over may be kept in the refrigerator for 3 days.

Sandwiches

Take fresh wholemeal bread, sliced; or soft rolls, halved. Spread with vegan margarine and filling of choice. Wrap in greaseproof paper or cling film to keep moist. Keep in a cool place.

Sandwich Fillings

Avocado pear
Mashed with lemon juice, a little French dressing, and chopped salted almonds.

Dried Fruit
Dates, raisins or sultanas, chopped or minced and added to chopped nuts with a little vegan salad dressing (p.78).

Fruits
Fresh fruit such as pineapple, peach, pear, etc., sliced with a little vegan salad dressing (p.78).

Miso Spreads of various flavours (p.17–18).

Peanut Butter
To this may be added sliced pineapple, chopped celery, chopped walnuts, or even strawberry jam.

Salads
Lettuce, cucumber, watercress and other salads are attractive.

Tomatoes
Sliced with finely chopped pickles and a little French dressing (p.77).

Sandwiches may be toasted. Vegan margarine should be spread on the outside to prevent the bread burning before the filling is heated.

Hot fillings may be placed on toast.

Scrambled Tofu

> 1 onion
> ½ lb tofu
> yeast extract
> salt, pepper
> 1 clove garlic, crushed
> 2 oz vegetable oil
> soya sauce
> pinch of turmeric

Chop the onion. Fry in hot oil with the garlic until soft. Add the salt, pepper, yeast extract and soya sauce to taste. Add a pinch of turmeric to give colour. Add the tofu and fry until brown.

Pitta Bread

For recipe, see p.113.

Trim the edge off one side and open the pitta bread like an envelope. Spread inside with vegan margarine. Fill the inside with a sandwich filling or fresh salad and dressing.

Variation:

Spread inside with vegan margarine and yeast extract, fill with cucumber and tomatoes, sliced, stoned olives or capers, and crumbled tofu. Grill until golden brown and heated through.

Afters

2–4 oz of tropical fruit mix

This is made up of dried fruit and nuts and seeds. It is easier and cheaper to buy this ready-made from a whole-food shop than to make it yourself.

Dried fruit
Such as peach or pear halves, banana chips, or a variety of nuts.

Any fresh fruit.

The Main Meal

The main meal of the day needs to be filling. For this reason a good helping of potatoes, rice, pasta in its various forms, or bread must be served. With this can be served any nutritious savoury dish and a vegetable or salad to add colour and texture.

Potatoes

Potatoes can be baked, boiled, mashed, roasted or fried in deep or shallow fat.

Baked

Choose medium-sized old potatoes and scrub clean, remove any eyes and prick the skin to prevent them bursting in the oven. Place them at the top of the oven, 400°F, 200°C, Mk 6, for ¾–1½ hrs depending on the size. Cut in half and spread with vegan margarine, or top with a savoury filling.

Boiled

Wash or scrape new potatoes, peel old potatoes. Cut into even-sized pieces and place in a pan of cold water, add salt if required. Bring to the boil and simmer with the lid on for 15–20 mins until tender.

Creamed Mashed Potatoes

Boil old potatoes and drain. Mash with a potato-masher or a fork until there are no lumps. Mix in 1 oz of vegan margarine and a little soya milk, season to taste and reheat before serving.

Roasted

Peel old potatoes and cut them into even-sized pieces and boil for 5 mins. Drain. Brush with vegetable oil and place in a roasting pan with a little oil, at the top of the oven, 425°F, 220°C, Mk 7, for 40 mins, turning once.

Fried

Peel old potatoes and cut them into thin slices for crisps or ¼ inch sticks for chips. Wash and dry the potatoes. Heat the vegetable oil until hot. Shallow-fry the crisps until brown, deep-fry the chips until crisp and brown. Remove form the oil and drain on absorbent paper.

Serve hot with no lid on the dish.

Rice

There are several varieties of rice. White and brown rice both come in three sizes – long- , medium- and short-grained. Long-grained is used in savoury dishes and salads. Medium-grained is used for stuffings. Short-grained is used in puddings.

Cooking the rice

Allow 2 oz of uncooked rice per person, this is roughly ⅓ of a cup. For 1 cup of rice allow 2 cups of water or stock and ½ tsp of salt. Bring the salted water to the boil, add the rice and stir until the water returns to the boil. Cover with the lid and boil for 10–15 mins until the water is absorbed and the rice is soft. Stir with a fork to separate the grains. Serve hot or cold. Brown rice takes ½–1½ times as long again to cook depending on the type of rice. Cooked rice will keep for 3 days in the refrigerator.

Pasta

The basis for pasta is flour from a hard durum wheat. The flour is mixed with oil and water, though *beware*: some pasta contains egg. Pasta may be white or coloured green with spinach purée. The pasta is dried long before being sold. There are more than thirty different types of pasta on the market. This is due to the moulding, which can be in long threads, tubes, or strips, of different thicknesses and shapes. The best known include noodles, spaghetti, lasagne, macaroni, and vermicelli.

Cooking the pasta

Most pasta is boiled. Allow 2 oz pasta per person. Place 1 tsp salt in 1 pt water and bring to the boil. Add the pasta to the boiling water and bring back to the boil. Do not break the long strands but rather lower them gently into the water, allowing them to soften and bend until they are covered. Cooking time depends on the type of pasta being used and can be from 3–20 mins. The pasta is cooked when it is soft to bite. Drain thoroughly and add a knob of vegan margarine or 1 Tblsp of olive oil and toss.

Pulses

Dried pulses are peas, beans, and lentils. If you wish to use them in a meal a little forethought is needed as they must be soaked beforehand. Place them in a large bowl, cover with water and allow them to soak overnight; or pour boiling water over them and leave to soak for 2 hrs. Drain. Place in a saucepan of water, add salt, 1 tsp per ½ lb pulses, and bring to the boil. Cover. Simmer as follows:

peas: ½ hour   **split peas:** ½ hour
butter beans: 1 hour   **haricot beans:** ¾ hour
lentils: ½ hour

They can be served hot, puréed with vegan margarine and seasoning; or cold, tossed in French dressing (p.77). They can be put in soups, stews, main dishes or salads.

Kidney beans

Do not use the water that the beans have soaked or boiled in for stock as it contains harmful chemicals. Allow the kidney beans to boil rapidly for at least 10 mins before simmering for the required time until soft. Always cook the kidney beans separately then add them to the dish 10 mins before serving.

Most pulses can be bought pre-cooked in tins. This is more expensive but saves time and effort.

Chickpeas in Soya Sauce

> 2 oz chickpeas
> 1 Dsp vegetable oil
> 1 small onion, chopped
> 1 Tblsp soya sauce

Soak, then cook the chickpeas. Heat the oil and fry the onion. Add the cooked chickpeas. Add the soya sauce and cook until it is absorbed.

Serve hot or cold.

Refried Red Kidney Beans

        2 oz red kidney beans, pre-cooked
        1 onion, chopped
        1 clove garlic, crushed
        1 Tblsp vegetable oil
        1 oz vegan margarine
        ½ tsp chilli powder
        salt, pepper

Fry onion and garlic in oil for 5 mins. Add margarine and beans.
Mash all together with a fork, stir in chilli powder and seasoning. Continue to fry for 15 mins until crisp.
    Serve with mashed potatoes or on toast.

Spicy Cauliflower

        1 small cauliflower
        1 oz desiccated coconut
        ¼ pt boiling water
        1 Dsp vegetable oil
        1 oz vegan margarine
        ½ tsp cumin
        ½ tsp chilli powder
        ½ tsp turmeric
        ½ tsp coriander
        ½ tsp ground ginger
        1 clove garlic, crushed
        1 tsp mustard seeds
        2 spring onions, chopped
        1 oz sultanas
        ¼ pt vegetable stock
        salt, pepper to taste

Soak the coconut in boiling water. Break cauliflower into florets.
Heat the oil and margarine, add all spices and cook gently until
mustard seeds start to pop. Add cauliflower florets, spring
onions, sultanas and stock. Strain the liquid off the coconut and
add it to the pan, discarding the coconut. Cover and cook for
10 mins. Season. Strain off the liquid and serve.

Bean Curry

> 1 oz butter beans
> 1 small onion, sliced
> 1 courgette, sliced
> ½ green pepper, sliced
> 1 oz mushrooms, sliced
> 1 clove garlic, crushed
> 1 Tblsp vegetable oil
> 1 oz raisins
> 1 Dsp cornflour
> 1 tsp curry powder
> ½ tsp ground ginger
> ½ pt vegetable stock
> salt, pepper to taste

Soak beans overnight and drain. Place in a pan of salted water and boil rapidly for 10 mins and drain again. Fry onions, courgette, pepper, mushrooms and garlic in oil for 5 mins. Add raisins, cornflour, spices, seasoning, beans and stir in the stock. Cover and simmer for 20 mins. Serve with rice or spaghetti.

Celery in Tomato Sauce

> ½ head celery
> 1 small tin tomatoes
> 1 small onion, grated
> 1 Tblsp tomato ketchup
> 1 tsp yeast extract
> 1 bay leaf
> ½ oz vegan margarine
> salt, pepper

Trim the celery. Cook gently, covered in boiling salt water until tender. Cook tinned tomatoes, yeast extract, onion, ketchup and bay leaf for 10 mins until the mixture is reduced and thickened. Remove the bay leaf. Drain the celery head and coat with margarine. Season. Place on serving dish and cover with the tomato mixture.

Fruit and Nut Risotto

   1 oz raisins
   1 oz cashew nuts, *or* any nuts
   2 oz cooked rice
   1 Tblsp vegan oil
   1 small onion, chopped
   ½ green pepper, chopped
   2 oz mushrooms, sliced
   1 tomato, chopped
   salt, pepper to taste

Heat the oil, add the onions and fry until soft. Add the peppers, nuts and mushrooms and cook for 5 mins. Add the rice, tomatoes, raisins and season to taste. Stir fry for 3 mins.

Serve hot with a salad.

Marrow with Mushroom Sauce

   ½ marrow
   ¼ pt water *or* stock
   salt
   1 tsp parsley, chopped
   ½ oz vegan margarine
   1 small onion, chopped
   2 oz mushrooms, chopped
   1 bay leaf

   White Sauce
   ½ oz vegan margarine
   1 oz flour
   ½ pt soya milk *or* stock *or* water
   salt, pepper
   1 tsp yeast extract

Peel the marrow, remove the pips. Cut into large cubes. Cook them in salted water or stock until tender, 5–10 mins. Drain. Sprinkle with parsley.

To make the sauce: melt the margarine in a pan and add the flour. Cook for 2 minutes. Add the milk or stock, stir continuously to prevent lumps. Stir gently until sauce thickens. Add the seasoning.

Heat the margarine and cook the onions and mushrooms for

2 mins. Add the sauce and bay leaf and stir all together. Cook for a further 2 mins.

Pour mushroom sauce over the marrow cubes to serve.

Paella

> 2 oz rice
> 1 Tblsp vegetable oil
> 1 small onion, chopped
> 1 garlic clove, crushed
> ¼ tsp turmeric powder
> a mixture of any vegetables, cleaned and chopped, about
>   ¼ lb
> ½ pt vegetable stock
> 1 Dsp parsley, chopped
> ½ tsp marjoram
> 1 Tblsp cashew nuts *or* any nuts
> juice and rind of ½ lemon
> 1 Dsp soya sauce
> salt, pepper

Fry rice in oil until golden. Add onions, garlic and turmeric and fry for 3 mins. Add all the vegetables and stock and bring to the boil. Simmer until the rice is cooked. Stir in herbs, nuts, lemon rind and juice, soya sauce and season to taste.

Serve hot.

Potatoes, Chickpeas and Tomatoes

> ½ lb potatoes
> 1 oz chickpeas, soaked
> 1 onion, thickly sliced
> 1 Dsp tomato purée
> ¼ pt water
> 1 clove garlic, crushed
> 1 Tblsp vegetable oil
> 1 Dsp tomato purée
> salt, pepper

Peel and slice potatoes thickly. Fry onions in oil until golden. Add drained chickpeas and garlic, fry in oil until brown. Add potatoes and turn them until they are brown. Add tomatoes,

tomato purée and water to cover. Season to taste. Bring to the
boil and simmer until the potatoes and chickpeas are soft.

May be served hot or cold.

Ratatouille

Try ratatouille (see recipe, p.47) – a delicious stew of vegetables
which adds colour to a meal, and can be served hot over
potatoes, rice and pasta. It is also delicious cold. Left-overs can
be mashed and added to gravy. It is easier to cook ratatouille in
bulk, but tinned ratatouille can be bought at a reasonable price.

Vegetable Crumble

1 small onion, sliced
1 stick celery, chopped
1 carrot, chopped
2 oz cooked peas
½ small cauliflower
1 Tblsp vegetable oil
½ oz flour
½–¾ pt water
1 Tblsp tahini
salt, pepper

Topping
½ oz vegan margarine
1 Dsp oil
2 oz flour
1 oz sesame seeds

Heat the oil in a pan and fry the onion, celery and carrot for 5
mins. Sprinkle in the flour and cook gently. Add the water
stirring continuously. Bring to the boil stirring until the sauce
thickens. Keep the sauce thick but runny by adding water if
necessary.

Break cauliflower into florets and add, simmer for 5 mins.
Add peas, tahini and seasoning. Stir. Transfer to a small
ovenproof dish.

Rub the margarine and oil into the flour until well mixed and like crumbs. Add the sesame seeds. Sprinkle the mixture evenly over the vegetables. Bake for 20 mins at 400°F, 200°C, Mk 6.

Serve hot with potatoes.

Vegetable Tart

Casing
6 oz 'Jus Rol' shortcrust pastry
2 oz dried peas *or* beans

Filling
1 stick celery
1 carrot
1 oz cauliflower
1 oz peas
1 oz beans
1 small onion, chopped
½ oz vegan margarine

White Sauce
1 Tblsp flour
½ oz vegan margarine
1 tsp yeast extract
salt, pepper
½ cup soya milk *or* stock *or* water

Roll the pastry out to ¼ inch thick and line a small tart dish. Cover base with dried peas and bake 'blind' in a hot oven 400°F, 200°C, Mk 6 for 15 mins.

Wash and peel the vegetables. Chop the carrot, celery and beans, divide the cauliflower into florets. Fry the onion and carrots in the fat for 6 mins. Boil the other vegetables until nearly soft, about 10 mins. Drain. Mix vegetables together and pour into the tart case.

Make a sauce by gently frying the flour for 1 min in the margarine, add the fluid stirring continuously until the sauce thickens. Add yeast extract and seasoning to taste.

Pour over the vegetables. Bake in oven 400°F, 200°C, Mk 6, for 20 mins.

Salads

Salads are an attractive accompaniment to any main dish (see pp.63–76).

Desserts

A pudding is not necessary if an adequate helping of the first course has been eaten but for those with a sweet tooth who like to round the meal off, here are a few simple recipes.

Custard

> 1 Tblsp custard powder
> ½ pt soya milk
> 1 Dsp sugar

Use a little of the soya milk to dissolve custard powder and sugar. Heat the remaining soya milk to almost boiling, add the dissolved custard powder and stir until it thickens.

Custard is delicious warm or cold on its own, or poured over a pudding.

Sliced banana, passion fruit, or mandarins are lovely added to custard.

Custard Fool

This can be made by whisking any puréed soft fruit into the custard, e.g. Stewed apple, stewed gooseberries, raspberries.

Fruit Salad

Take 3 types of fruit as a base, e.g. Apples, pears, oranges or bananas, grapefruit and plums. Prepare them by segmenting, slicing or dicing finely. To the base add one exotic fruit in season, e.g. Strawberries halved, cherries destoned, kiwi fruit sliced, firm raspberries. Pour over a pure fruit juice. Serve on its own with a sprig of mint to decorate or accompanied with custard or coconut cream.

Stewed Apple

Peel, core and slice one large cooking apple. Place in a saucepan with 1 Tblsp water and simmer with the lid on for 5 mins. Add 1 Dsp of sugar to taste, ¼ tsp of ground cinnamon, ¼ tsp ground cloves and ¼ tsp of nutmeg. Serve hot or cold, with custard or on cereals.

1 Dsp of raisins added with the sugar will give extra texture and colour.

Index

(* Suitable for entertaining non-vegans)